BEST REGION

BOULDER
HIKING TRAILS

Bette Erickson

PHOTOGRAPHY BY
Russell and Gail Dohrmann

WESTCLIFFE PUBLISHERS
www.bigearthpublishing.com

ISBN 978-1-56579-522-8
Text copyright: Bette Erickson, 2005. All rights reserved. Updated 2009.
Photography copyright: Russell and Gail Dohrmann, 2005. All rights reserved.
Editor: Kate Hawthorne
Designer: Angie Lee, Grindstone Graphics
Production Manager: Carol Pando

Published by:
Westcliffe Publishers
a Big Earth Publishing company
1637 Pearl Street, Suite 201
Boulder, CO 80302

Printed in China
Library of Congress Cataloging-in-Publication Data:
Erickson, Bette.
  Best Boulder-Region hiking trails / Bette Erickson ; photography by Russell and Gail Dohrmann.
    p. cm.
  Includes bibliographical references and index.
  ISBN-13: 978-1-56579-522-8
  ISBN-10: 1-56579-522-9
  1. Hiking—Colorado—Boulder Region—Guidebooks. 2. Trails—Colorado—Boulder Region—Guidebooks. 3. Boulder Region (Colo.)—Guidebooks. I. Title.
  GV199.42.C62B6845 2005
  917.88'63—dc22
                                2004027899

For more information about other fine books and calendars from Westcliffe Publishers, a Big Earth Publishing company, please contact your local book-store, call us at 1-800-523-3692, write for our free color catalog, or visit us on the web at **wbigearthpublishing.com.**

Title Page: Calypso Cascade, Bluebird Lake Trail, Wild Basin area
Opposite: Bierstadt Trail, Bear Lake area

Please Note: Risk is always a factor in backcountry and high-mountain travel. Many of the activities described in this book can be dangerous, especially when weather is adverse or unpredictable, and when unforeseen events or conditions create a hazardous situation. The author has done her best to provide the reader with accurate information about backcoun-try travel, as well as to point out some of its potential hazards. It is the responsibility of the users of this guide to learn the necessary skills for safe backcountry travel, and to exercise caution in potentially hazardous areas, especially on glaciers and avalanche-prone terrain. The author and publisher disclaim any liability for injury or other damage caused by back-country traveling or performing any other activity described in this book.

Acknowledgments

This book would not have been possible without the assistance of many people. I am most grateful to my husband and hiking partner, Paul Beaty. I always rely on Paul's strength, intelligence, and integrity. Paul likes to hike for the fun of it. I am indebted to him for his support while I researched and hiked all of the trails for this book.

A thank you is due to our son and daughter, Greg and Haley. Although they are away at college and obviously busy, they both took the time to skim over the manuscript and offer some valuable insight and typically sassy remarks.

Thanks, also, are due to Westcliffe Publishers' John Fielder, Linda Doyle, Martha Gray, Carol Pando, and Jenna Browning, for their shared foresight in the creation of this work. And particularly a heartfelt thank you to editor extraordinaire Kate Hawthorne.

A huge thank you is owed to photographers Russell and Gail Dohrmann, who painstakingly captured so beautifully the essence of the trails.

Thanks go to Tina Nielsen and Pascale Fried with Boulder County Parks and Open Space. Additional thanks go to Dave Sutherland and Cathy Vaughan-Grabowski with the City of Boulder Open Space & Mountain Parks. Mark Holst and Bill Newman with Rocky Mountain National Park were accommodating to me in my fact-finding efforts. Maribeth Pecotte at the Boulder Ranger District of the U.S. Forest Service was helpful as well.

Thank you to my friend Carey Fuller, who enjoys hiking as much as I do and consistently offered his encouragement, although I could rarely keep his pace hiking.

And finally, my sincere gratitude and deep respect is offered to those who have planned these trails, hiked them, and maintained the areas I wrote about.

In Memoriam
Robert Winston Erickson
(1914–1967)
Clara Lucille Augustine
(1922–1994)

To Paul, Greg, and Haley—you are the best part of my life.

Bluebell-Baird Trail, City of Boulder
Open Space & Mountain Parks

Contents

Mountains

Introduction

The trail up Green Mountain weaves through forests, connects with other routes, and cuts past rocky outcrops, ultimately leading to one of the best views overlooking the City of Boulder. It was one of the first hikes I did with my soon-to-be husband many, many years ago.

Trying to impress him, I challenged him to a race back to the trailhead. Midway down the mountain I heard him call my name. As I quickly turned, I rested my hand on what I thought was a rock behind me. It was a huge cactus. We spent the next 20 minutes picking inch-long thorns out of the palm of my hand. One of us felt the need to make wisecracks while doing that.

The purpose of this guidebook is to share with you my love of hiking and being outdoors. I hope to capture the spirit of adventure that mountain hiking provides. People of all ages can be sustained and rejuvenated by the highlands for a day, a few weeks, or even a lifetime; none of us is too young to begin, or too old to participate.

Boulder has always been a city that has attracted idealists and visionaries—a town founded on the glimmer of gold and the promise of better days. While Boulder's destiny was originally shaped by geology—silver, gold, and other natural resources—the city continues to attract modern settlers seeking a better life, primarily because of its magnificent landscape. Pioneered by farmers, miners, and even gold diggers, the city has evolved since its founding in 1859, identifying the importance of environmental protection, education, and quality of life issues.

Boulder has successfully insulated itself against metropolitan sprawl with a ring of mountain parks and green space. The city is surrounded by thousands of acres of city-owned open space lands that are undoubtedly some of the most scenic and diverse in the country. Hiking in Boulder yields immense satisfaction, particularly because of the planning and forethought that went into creating and maintaining this beautiful setting.

The hiking here takes you by surprise. One moment you're walking on the quiet, tree-lined streets of the hip, college town and then—seemingly just a decision later—you're buried in the forest's ruggedness. I enjoy hiking in and around Boulder because of the open spaces, unsurpassed panoramic views, and the many interesting, health-conscious people.

Some of the best hiking is usually done with family or friends. Most often these days my husband and I hike together without our two children, or our sweet little dog, Disney. A couple of times a summer, however, our son and daughter will accompany us up a mountain, a tradition that began many

Water flow and Parry primrose,
Diamond Lake Trail, Hessie Townsite area

> **"There's a long, long trail a-winding into the land of my dreams...."**
>
> *—Song writer Stoddard King*

years ago. When the children were preschoolers, their idea of a mountain hike was finding the nearest big rock and sitting down for lunch.

Hiking supports all the elements of a great family outing: it is active, low-cost, and exciting. Several years ago we were making the nearly 2,500-foot vertical climb up Bear Peak in Boulder, and our daughter turned to me and asked, "Mom, have we made the Dairy Queen summit yet or the Oreo summit?" In our family, the DQ summit is truly the top of the mountain, whereas the Oreo summit is merely giving the mountain a good try and stopping at that point to eat cookies and assess our progress. Achieving the DQ summit yields a trip for ice cream on the way home.

We Westerners take quiet, empty horizon vistas for granted, but my friends and family visiting from big cities on the east and west coasts struggle to recognize silence and enjoy the unobstructed, panoramic landscape. I love being able to take visitors into the backcountry. To me, the experience is thrilling and as energizing as an elixir. Following a hike, I almost always return feeling rejuvenated, retuned, and restarted.

Personally, I'm a warm-weather hiker. There's really no substitute for scuffing up your hiking boots and discovering what all the fuss is about. Hiking across meadows bursting with wildflowers and strolling near tumbling streams and through shady woodlands is what makes summer hiking such a delight.

While the mountains are certainly lovely, they are not benign. Being prepared can make any hiking experience much more comfortable and perhaps help in a potentially threatening situation. I've encountered more bears, foxes, coyotes, and deer on and off trail than I can remember. Moreover, faster than you can zip your backpack and lace your hiking boots, Colorado's high country can have a rapid weather change.

Once, while my husband and I were descending Torreys Peak, about a thousand feet from the summit, a storm came in, plummeting violent rain on the mountain. Lightning strikes came as close to us as 300 yards. Thinking that we could take a faster shortcut down to get out of the storm, we and several others on the mountain that day left the trail: Never a good idea.

We came upon a large snowfield with no other option than to climb down very near and sometimes on the snow or backtrack an hour in the thundering rain. Before we got down into the treeline, the mountain was drenched and we were certain we had met our maker.

"The longest journey is the journey inwards," wrote Dag Hammarskjöld, former secretary-general of the United Nations. The trails I take lead outward into the hills and forests, but they lead inward as well. I always find God when I'm outdoors, deep in the woods, or high on a treeless mountain summit. That's why I hike. You can experience that serenity and peace even when hiking with a group.

I hope you enjoy this hiking guide as much as I've enjoyed putting it together. I've written it at the urging of my friends who take pleasure in hiking as much as I do.

Find your adventure. Be safe and be mindful of backcountry ethics. Anything is possible on an earth that creates for itself such a fabulous landscape of forests, lakes, and mountains.

—*Bette Erickson*
Broomfield, Colorado

Mount Toll reflected in Mitchell Lake, Indian Peaks Wilderness

How To Use This Guide

The Front Range of Colorado extends north from the Arkansas River Valley west of Pueblo to the Wyoming border, a length of about 175 picturesque miles. There are few places in the United States as diverse as our Front Range, from the dry, dusty tumbleweed-brushed high plains to the perennially snow-capped tips of the highest peaks.

This guidebook covers hikes that can be completed in one day or less in and around Boulder, Colorado, as well as the Indian Peaks Wilderness and Rocky Mountain National Park to the west of the city. My husband and I have actually hiked all of the 80 or so trails described in this guide, some favorite trails many times.

Parry primrose and spring runoff, Jean
Lunning Trail, Brainard Lake area

To help you select the type of hike you'd like to try, the guide is divided into three geographic areas: Flatlands, Foothills, and Mountains.

▼ **The flatlands** extend to an elevation of about 5,600 feet. Contrary to the name, the flatlands consist of rolling terrain and small ridges as well as the level, nearly treeless plains to the east of Boulder.

▼ **The foothills** are the transition between the flatlands and the mountains, approximately 5,500 to 8,000 feet in elevation. The slopes of the eastern foothills are covered in pines and fir, and offer some of the most popular hikes in the Boulder area.

▼ **The mountains** rise from the foothills to the Continental Divide. The highest point in Colorado is the windswept summit of Mount Elbert, at 14,433 feet above sea level. A total of 54 peaks in the state rise higher than 14,000 feet, dubbed fourteeners by hiking and climbing enthusiasts. Challenging, breathtakingly beautiful hikes can be found throughout the high country west of Boulder.

More than 31,600 acres of publicly accessible open space lands surround the city. In Boulder, the park system represents a marvelous diversity of scenic wonders: towering flatirons, vast canyon lands, and icy streams rushing down from higher elevations. It also serves a diversity of outdoor aficionados: hikers, runners, mountain bikers, equestrians, and others. Trail courtesies include staying right as you make your way along routes to avoid collisions with oncoming traffic.

Our federal, state, and local tax dollars help pay for these open spaces and remote places presented in this guidebook. I have included hikes in areas under the jurisdiction of Boulder County Parks and Open Space, and City of Boulder Open Space & Mountain Parks. Indian Peaks Wilderness and Rocky Mountain National Park are managed by the U.S. Forest Service and National Park Service.

Hike Listings

Each hike presents essential facts at a glance:

To the trailhead:	Detailed driving directions from within the City of Boulder
Distance:	Approximate mileage of the hike in round-trip totals, unless otherwise noted
Difficulty:	Easy, moderate, or strenuous. These hikes are suitable for the average, reasonably fit hiker; adjustments may be necessary for individual abilities
Elevation gain:	Vertical feet gained. This gives an idea how steep the trail is, and is an important factor to consider when choosing a hike, because a 1.5-mile trail with 1,000 feet elevation gain could be perceived as more strenuous than a 3-mile trail with the same rise in elevation. Where trails begin and end at roughly the same elevation, the gain is negligible, unless the terrain varies greatly in between.
Dogs:	Whether dogs are allowed on the trails. Dog rules vary depending on area, but always include picking up after your pet. Check with the appropriate jurisdiction to see if dogs are allowed before you make the trip with your canine friend.
Highlights:	Some of the things that make each hike special
Jurisdiction:	The land management agency to which you report an incident or to contact if you have questions before you begin your outing. (A complete list of land management contacts is listed in Appendix B, p. 261.)

The maps pictured in this book are for route definition only; it is suggested that updated, full-scale USGS quadrangles or other detailed maps be obtained before visiting an area. Whether visiting a national, state, or local park, be sure to carry a trail map, and study it so you can accurately select the best hike for you and your family. An excellent variety of tear-resistant, waterproof, all-inclusive maps are available at local booksellers. And be sure to study the posted map at the trailhead kiosk, if available, before you begin your outing.

Wildflowers, Bluebird Lake Trail, Wild Basin area

For the purpose of this guidebook, I've made every attempt to be as specific as possible when describing how to get to a trailhead. However, trailhead locations change or trails get rerouted. At the time of this publication, all trails were verified as accurate. Please feel free to contact the publisher about any mistakes, updates, or suggestions.

Be Prepared

Please keep in mind that anything can happen while in the backcountry. The weather turning worse, getting lost, encounters with wildlife, or even injury— all have happened to me and my hiking partners at one time or another. Never hike alone, and let someone know where you are going and when you expect to return. Where available, sign in at the trailhead register before departing.

Being prepared is really very simple. When I have the opportunity to steal into the sunshine for a day hike, I carry the following hiking essentials with me:

▼ A backpack with zippered compartments

▼ Details of the area (map, directions to trailhead)

▼ Plenty of drinking water

▼ Energy bars, fruit and/or peanuts, and definitely chocolate

▼ A compass (and know how to use it)

▼ Sunglasses, hat, and sunscreen

▼ A small first aid kit

▼ Flashlight, extra sweater, gloves, rain poncho

▼ Camera

▼ Identification (driver's license)

Obviously if it's a casual stroll in a city park you don't need all those supplies. But in the backcountry, the above list offers basics that you may find useful. For the most part, hiking in the mountains is safe and immensely pleasurable—if you use caution and common sense.

When hiking with children, consider their ages and the length of the trail, the ease or difficulty of the terrain, and the sights along the way. Hiking with the intent of finding a waterfall, a scenic view, or interesting landmark is a good incentive. And, of course, be sure everyone is prepared with plenty of water, snacks, and comfortable hiking boots.

When hiking fourteeners, it's wise to be at the trailhead well before sunrise. During July and August, it is vitally important to be off the summit around noon or one o'clock, when afternoon electrical storms can predictably set in.

Opposite: Alpine meadow, Devil's Thumb Lake Trail, Jasper Lake area

Be Respectful

The city parks, trails, mountains, and open spaces outlined here are diverse and beautiful. We are lucky that many of our municipal parks and open space departments work hard to purchase and preserve open lands. But these are also fragile treasures. We must continue to educate ourselves extensively about the ecosystems of our Colorado landscape so that we do not damage it unintentionally out of ignorance. Common sense and courtesy ought to guide our behavior.

Please don't pick the flowers while enjoying the outdoors, whether you're in the flatlands, foothills, or mountains. To protect yourself and preserve the environment, leave flora intact for the next visitor to enjoy. Moreover, as tempting as it is, don't feed the squirrels or Canada geese, either. They won't have your bread crusts or cashews to enjoy during the long, cold winter months. By not feeding the wildlife, it helps encourage the critters to remain self-reliant.

Whether we are in a remote wilderness or a bustling city park, we must embrace the ethics that allow us to Leave No Trace. That means plan ahead, leave what you find, pick up after yourself and others, and respect wildlife. For instance, when photographing wildlife, if you think you're too close, you probably are, particularly if the animal(s) appear frightened or confused. Remember: "Take nothing but pictures; leave nothing but footprints."

For a list of specifics regarding outdoor ethics and Leave No Trace, visit www.LNT.org for more information (see Appendix B, p. 261).

**Opposite: Bear Peak, Walter
Orr Roberts Trail, NCAR Mesa**

Regional Map

Regions

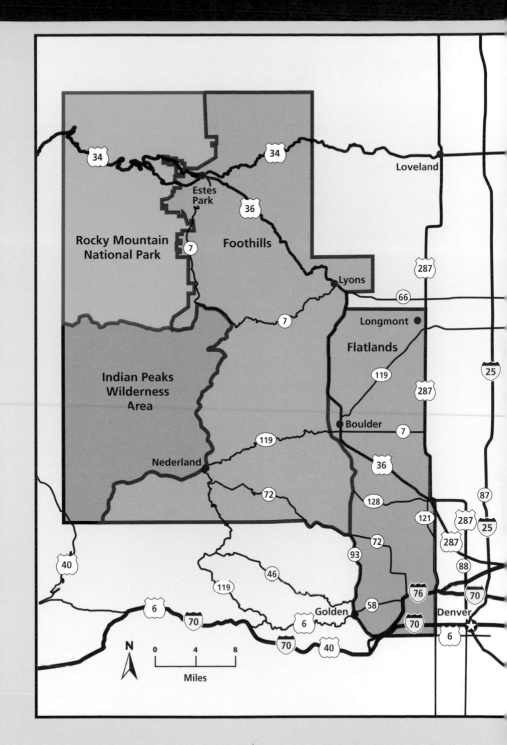

Flatlands

More than a century has passed since the Gold Rush of 1858 lured thousands upon thousands of fortune-seeking folks to the Front Range of the Rockies. Many generations have since stayed, settling along the flatlands, foothills, and in the mountains. They spent decades raising families and calling Colorado home.

> "Though we travel the world over to find the beautiful, we must carry it with us or we find it not."
>
> —*Ralph Waldo Emerson*

Making up two-fifths of the state, the flatlands are vast and nearly treeless plains east of the Rocky Mountains. Of the trees that are native, the cottonwoods and willows are found along streams and rivers, drinking up moisture that comes infrequently to Colorado's lower elevations. Vegetation found along the plains includes native grasses such as timothy and foxtail barley.

Contents

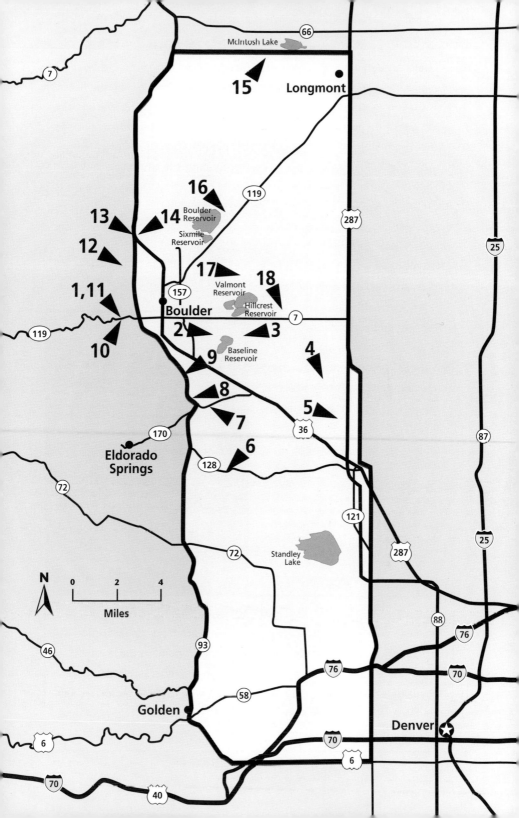

McIntosh Lake

66

15

Longmont

7

119

287

25

16

13

14

Boulder
Reservoir

12

Sixmile
Reservoir

17

Valmont
Reservoir

18

1, 11

157

Boulder

Hillcrest
Reservoir

10

119

2

3

7

4

9

Baseline
Reservoir

8

5

7

36

170

6

Eldorado
Springs

128

72

121

287

87

25

72

Standley
Lake

88

76

N

0   2   4

46

Miles

93

76

70

6

58

Golden

Denver

6

40

70

70

70

6

Decades ago, cities put forth a concerted effort to plant more trees throughout the Boulder Valley Great Plains grasslands. Trees or not, the flatlands support most of the sprawling urban population that slowly and steadily thrusts out of the region's eastern boundary, as urbanism's tendrils continue to extend. Yet in Boulder, the commitment of limiting urban sprawl is evident by its ring of dedicated open space lands surrounding the city. Numerous trails weave in and around Boulder, intersecting and connecting to routes leading to neighboring municipalities as well as destinations within the city. These planned and maintained trails, in addition to providing recreational uses, also allow many residents to commute to work via bicycling and hiking.

A hike along the flatlands is nearly always a possibility (weather permitting) on an otherwise busy day. Regional parks and pocket parks throughout Boulder are open from sunrise to sunset. As you hike in the flatlands, keep an eye out for golden eagles, jackrabbits, badgers, rats, fox, larks, prairie dogs, and falcons. In areas where fishing is permitted, a state fishing license is generally required for anglers 16 years and older.

The following hikes are suitable for all ages and abilities.

Summer meadow,
Coulson Gulch Trail, Big Elk
Meadows Wildflowers

Tall Tale

The mean elevation of Colorado is 6,800 feet, earning it the distinction of being the highest state in the country. The lowest point in the state is where the Arkansas River flows into Kansas at an altitude of 3,350 feet. The altitude of the City of Boulder is at 5,430 feet, keeping temperatures cool at night even on scorching summer days. Gentle mountain winds and low precipitation help, too.

Boulder Creek Path

Weaving through the hip college town of Boulder, the cottonwood-shaded Boulder Creek Path is a favorite for runners, cyclists, walkers, and people-watchers.

Fall cottonwoods, Bobolink Trail, Boulder County Parks and Open Space

Dotted with public art and historical interpretive markers, the lengthy 7-mile trail is beautiful in all seasons. Stops along the way include the Boulder Public Library, Central Park at the southeast corner of Broadway and Canyon, Scott Carpenter Park, and, of course, the creek itself, particularly during the spring runoff.

During the spring and summer, kids and adults drift down the cold creek on inner tubes and kayaks. I find it immensely pleasurable to watch the younger children as they squeal and giggle, making their way into the icy water.

Because of its popularity, most of the trail is paved. In the canyon to the west, at the Elephant Buttress area, the trail becomes crusher-fine gravel.

On 6th Street, the community demonstration xeriscape garden is a good place to learn about water-saving plants. A child's fishing pond and sculpture garden is located just west of 9th Street, and The International Peace Garden can be found near the Boulder Public Library. But that's not all. It's a busy trail with lots of interesting spurs and diversions.

The Boulder Creek Path parallels the creek through town, connecting in various locations along what's known as the Boulder Greenway system.

Near the junction of Boulder and Fourmile Canyons, the Boulder Creek Path ends at the old townsite of Orodell, a long-ago mining town that bustled with activity during the 1870s.

Boulder Creek, Boulder Creek Path, City of Boulder

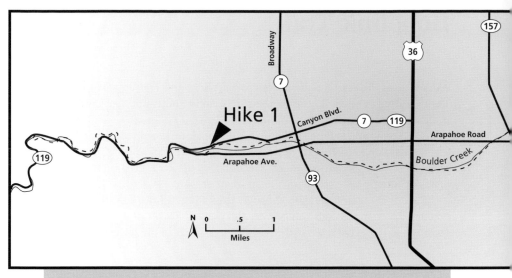

To the trailhead: Access to the Boulder Creek Path is available from many points throughout the city. A good west access is at Eben G. Fine Park (see Hike 10, p. 50); from Broadway (CO 93), go west on Arapahoe Ave. approximately 2 miles to the mouth of Boulder Canyon. Another good access is at Scott Carpenter Park on the southwest corner of Arapahoe Road and 30th St., east of the intersection with 28th St. (US 36).

Distance: 7 miles one-way

Difficulty: Easy to moderate depending on distance traveled

Elevation gain: 600 feet from its east end near Valmont Lake to its western end at Fourmile Canyon Drive.

Dogs: On leash only

Highlights: A wide, popular trail paralleling the creek through the heart of the city

Jurisdiction: City of Boulder Parks and Recreation along the 5.5 miles in the innermost city; Boulder County Parks and Open Space from the Elephant Buttress area to where the trail terminates in Fourmile Canyon. (Contact information for each jurisdiction can be found in Appendix A, p. 260.)

Bobolink Trail

Any time of the year is a good time to visit Bobolink Trail in east Boulder. The expertly groomed, 3.5-mile path skirts along South Boulder Creek and is a part of the extensive ever-linking Boulder trail system.

The scenic and serene trail offers a seasonal, lush, wetland environment for runners, cyclists, hikers, and equestrians as well as wildlife. If you're lucky, you can expect to see deer, raccoons, or maybe even a salamander near the water.

Part of the trail meanders through the Tallgrass Prairie Natural Area, populated with indigenous wildflowers and grasses. Raptor nests and craggy cottonwood trees characterize the path leading south to the town of Marshall.

Boulder foothills and cottonwoods, near Bobolink Trail

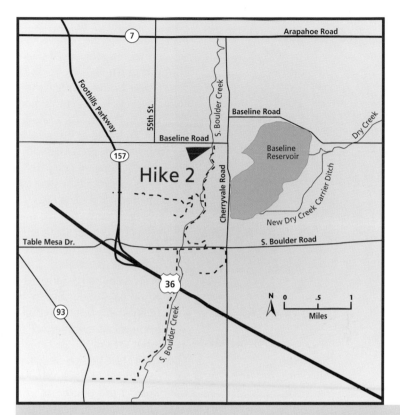

To the trailhead: From the intersection of Broadway CO 93 and Baseline Road, go east on Baseline to Cherryvale Road. Take the first left past the southernmost intersection of Baseline and Cherryvale Roads to the clearly marked Bobolink Trailhead and its large parking area.

Distance: 7 miles round-trip

Difficulty: Easy

Elevation gain: Negligible

Dogs: On leash only; not permitted on the southern end of the trail where indicated

Highlights: Trail rambles through lush riparian and grassland ecosystems

Jurisdiction: City of Boulder Open Space & Mountain Parks

Wild iris

Begin by going directly south from the trailhead on either the wide, paved walkway or through the packed gravel footpath among the trees, closer to South Boulder Creek. The trails are parallel.

In less than 0.5 mile or so, you'll be presented with a choice: The concrete path loops around to the west over a footbridge leading elsewhere. However, for the purpose of this hike, stay south following the dirt footpath alongside the creek.

At about 1.5 miles, you'll pass under South Boulder Road, and the trail becomes a gravel service road. Veer right (west) for 0.3 mile. The Bobolink Trail runs alongside South Boulder Road at this point.

Remnants of the old Dorn Farm site are visible west of the path near the underpass.

Continue on, ultimately reaching an access gate, then turn left (south) for just less than 2 miles before reaching Marshall Road. At the time of this printing, dogs were not allowed south beyond the gate area.

Lakes and wetlands near Marshall Road allow for waterfowl viewing, perhaps even a rare glimpse of the bobolink, an American migratory songbird for which the trail was named. The site of the Abernathy Dairy can be seen to the east of the creek, where this trail dead-ends.

The pleasant Bobolink Trail, winding through riparian and grassland ecosystems, offers visitors a habitat mosaic that is unusual in the heart of Boulder.

Dry Creek Trail

Just east of Baseline Reservoir and Cherryvale Road is the broad Dry Creek Trail. The sublime surroundings offer unobstructed views of the Front Range to the west and allow visitors a peaceful retreat away from the hustle and bustle of downtown Boulder and the nearby University of Colorado campus.

The Dry Creek Trail is actually a loop: a short, level, and easy 1-mile route. To start the hike, walk along the wide, gravel path past the prairie dog town to your left, crossing Dry Creek on a small wooden footbridge. Immediately west of the creek, you may choose either branch of the loop.

The right side veers west and parallels the eastern shore of the private Baseline Reservoir. The left branch of the trail hugs Dry Creek. Each route has a sharp turn, connecting the top half of the loop to the west.

There is a social trail beyond the left (south) side of the loop that follows a fence line. It's not officially a trail extension, and should probably not be trampled on.

Dry Creek Trail, Boulder County
Parks and Open Space

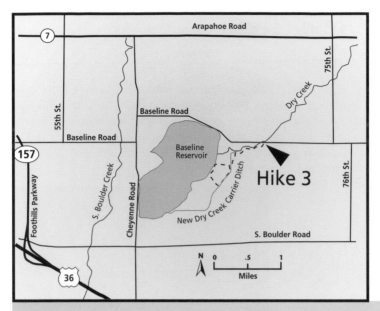

To the trailhead: Dry Creek Trailhead is located 0.5 mile east of Baseline Reservoir. From central Boulder, go east on Baseline Road to Cherryvale Road. Turn left (north) onto Cherryvale then right (east) onto Baseline again, continuing around the private Baseline Reservoir. The trailhead is on the south side of Baseline Road. Ample trailhead parking is available.

Distance: 1-mile loop

Difficulty: Easy

Elevation gain: Negligible

Dogs: Yes, under voice and sight command, or on leash; may not enter or disturb prairie dog colony

Highlights: A short, level loop, ideal for casual hikers

Jurisdiction: City of Boulder Open Space & Mountain Parks

The Dry Creek Trail is a wonderful jaunt that begins and ends over winding Dry Creek. Surprisingly remote in appearance and ambience, this is an ideal trail with little sense of overcrowding, attracting hikers and runners ready for a brief workout, friends catching up with each other, nature observers, and even the amorous, walking hand-in-hand.

Coal Creek Trail

As suburbs push against open space lands throughout the metro area, one example of a successful partnership between landowners and municipalities is the Coal Creek Trail. It is located between Louisville and Lafayette in eastern Boulder County. This trail links with Superior's Rock Creek and Coalton Trails and is a part of a 20-mile regional system linking the four towns of Superior, Louisville, Lafayette, and Boulder.

The 10-foot wide trail is mainly crusher-fine gravel with a few low spots paved with concrete. Part of the popular footpath winds through dense shrubs and is canopied with large cottonwood trees. However, other parts remain open, abutting a miscellaneous setting of pastoral lands, commerce, and residences.

If you're seeking a remote, away-from-it-all experience, this isn't it. Depending on the time of day or day of the week, the trail can be populated by a variety of people or by no one at all. On the other hand, if you're pressed for time and want somewhere to walk with your dog, bike, or run, this is a near perfect choice to add to your repertoire of urban trails. The route is suitable for folks in wheelchairs or youngsters in strollers.

Because of its negligible elevation gain with its rolling hills, it's also a good seasonal trail for cross-country skiing and snowshoeing.

Fall cottonwoods, Coal Creek Trail, Louisville

After parking at the Aquarius Trailhead, you may opt to go left (west) toward Louisville, with its uninterrupted views of the stern, blue-green Front Range, or take the right fork and head east toward Lafayette. This trailhead is at the center of a 7-mile, completely uninterrupted stretch.

The trailhead's small-group shelter is an ideal picnic gazebo, accommodating up to 20 people, on a first-come, first-serve basis. Because of the environmentally sensitive nature of the area, and the fact that the Coal Creek Trail consists in parts of an easement with property owners, visitors to the trail should be mindful of open space rules and regulations.

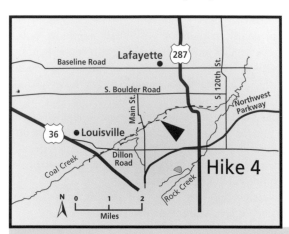

You may also access the Coal Creek Trail at its eastern third portion at the Avalon Trailhead located south of South Boulder Road just past Public Road in Lafayette.

To the trailhead:	Access the Coal Creek Trail via the Aquarius Trailhead located 1.4 miles west of US 287 on CO 42. From central Boulder, take Arapahoe Road (CO 7) east to 95th St. (CO 42). Turn right (south) and follow CO 42 around a wide bend to the east. The parking area is well marked.
Distance:	7 miles one-way
Difficulty:	Easy to moderate
Elevation gain:	Negligible
Dogs:	Yes, on leash
Highlights:	Wheelchair accessible; group shelter at trailhead
Jurisdiction:	Boulder County Parks and Open Space

Carolyn Holmberg Preserve at Rock Creek Farm

Mary Miller Trail, Rock Creek Farm, Carolyn Holmberg Preserve

Flatlands

A visit to the Rock Creek Farm includes sweeping mountain views and tranquil and earthy acreage kept in its natural state. With minimal development and an emphasis on preserving habitat for wildlife, it feels as if you've stepped back in time a couple of centuries. The 994-acre open space nestled between Louisville and Broomfield is named in memory of Carolyn Holmberg, director of Boulder County Parks and Open Space from 1983 to 1998. Holmberg is credited with preserving some 40,000 acres of farms, ranches, wetlands, and forests from development.

Much of the area surrounding the Carolyn Holmberg Preserve at Rock Creek Farm is leased to private enterprises for crop production and livestock grazing. The land was a farm during the 1859 gold rush, later purchased by Mary and Lafayette Miller. The Overland Mail Stage operated a Pony Express stop here in 1870.

**Grasses and trees, Stearns Lake,
Carolyn Holmberg Preserve**

Rock Creek Farm offers a tiny lake, glowing turquoise blue. Stearns Lake is a 25-acre pond, attracting grebes, cormorants, and herons during the summer, and migrating waterfowl during spring and fall. The lake is stocked with tiger muskie and channel catfish. While fishing is permitted, no boating is allowed.

Expect to see muskrats along the marshy shallows. The open space area is a popular habitat for great horned owls, magpies, kingfishers, raccoons, and numerous songbirds. Several large black-tailed prairie dog villages make up the area as well.

From the South 104th Street parking area, walk south through a gate onto a wide, flat, crushed-gravel trail that circles the northeast side of Stearns Lake.

To the trailhead:	Located at the southwest quadrant of US 287 and Dillon Road in Boulder County. From Boulder, take 28th St. (US 36) south to McCaslin Blvd. Go north to Dillon Road: turn right (east). Take Dillon Road 3.1 miles to 104th Street, on your right. Drive about 0.8 mile to the trailhead on your left.
Distance:	3.4 miles round-trip
Difficulty:	Easy
Elevation gain:	Negligible
Dogs:	Yes, on leash
Highlights:	Pubic facilities and picnic tables at trailhead; fishing permitted, but no boating
Jurisdiction:	Boulder County Parks and Open Space

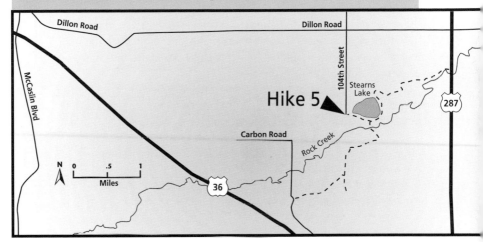

The trail will fork, eventually merging again, so it doesn't matter whether you choose to go right or left. Following the trail nearest the shoreline of Stearns Lake offers a constant view across open water and into the sandy lakeshore marshes.

Signs will indicate whether the wildlife areas on the west and north sides of the lake are open, allowing visitors to explore even farther off the footpath.

Following the trail north and east, you'll parallel a double fence line and cross open grassland that is pitted with prairie dogs burrows, eventually ending at a smaller parking lot on the south side of Dillon Road. Turn around and return the way you came.

Flatlands

Coalton Trail

On the fringes of suburban Boulder, the Coalton Trail is a convenient jaunt on back-from-the-past rangeland. The trail curves and bends on a moderate gradient where cacti bloom and wildlife roam. Equestrians and mountain bikers frequent this route, making it a true multi-use trail, but it is really an ideal runners' and hikers' trail. Formerly a two-track county road, its moderate, packed-gravel path winds through rolling grasslands near the town of Superior.

Expect to see coyotes trotting alongside the path during the early morning hours and to hear the familiar chirping of neighboring prairie dog colonies.

Starting at the parking area off of CO 128, the trail heads east. Be sure to close the gate behind you to keep occasional grazing livestock inside. You'll soon pass what appears to be an abandoned corral, wooden and weathered, on your right, adding to the charm of Coalton Trail.

The broad trail continues east, eventually curving northbound, passing artistic electrical towers and skirting alongside a barbed-wire fence the whole way. This relatively flat trail, a great path for an evening run or a quiet walk, is popular with cyclists as well. Of course, with the wonderful mountain backdrop to the west, the trek feels like a steady trip to remoteness, yet it's easy to keep your sense of direction.

It's occasionally nice to hike someplace where you don't get the sense that you are deeply buried in a forest, which contributes to the appeal of the Coalton

Flowers, Coalton
Trail, Boulder
County Parks and
Open Space

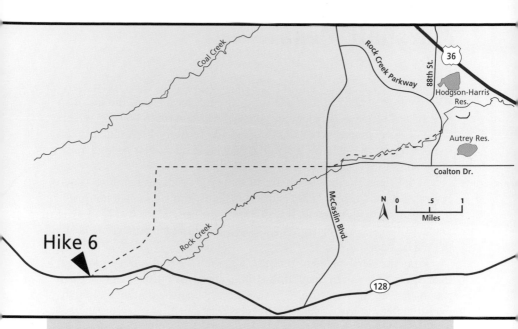

Hike 6

To the trailhead:	From Boulder, take Broadway (CO 93) south to CO 128. Turn left (east) and drive 2 miles to the Coalton Trailhead, on your left. To access the McCaslin side of the Coalton Trail, take US 36 south to McCaslin Blvd., turn right (south) and drive to where westbound Coalton Road dead-ends at McCaslin Blvd. in Superior.
Distance:	4 miles round-trip
Difficulty:	Easy
Elevation gain:	Rolling hills offering negligible elevation gain
Dogs:	Yes, on leash
Highlights:	Wide, packed-gravel path with sweeping mountain views
Jurisdiction:	Boulder County Parks and Open Space

Trail. The final leg of the 2-mile route takes a sharp right turn and veers east before spilling onto the trailhead at McCaslin Boulevard, where it ends.

The trail is accessible from either McCaslin Boulevard or CO 128. Whichever direction you choose, it's a great area for exercise, solitude, and fantastic mountain views.

Flatlands

Hike 7

Marshall Mesa

What once had been a rough and rowdy frontier town is now the site of a peaceful and scenic valley showcase. Marshall Mesa, in south Boulder, is home to the first coal mining activity in the Colorado Territory. Beginning in 1860 and continuing through the 1930s, Marshall provided coal for heating, railroads, and steam engines.

At one time, Marshall was home to some 900 residents and three saloons. Several spots on the trail offer historical markers with fascinating information regarding the settlement. It wasn't until the early 1970s that the City of Boulder Open Space & Mountain Parks department began purchasing land in this old coal mining area.

From the Marshall Mesa Trailhead, following the trail south for just less than a mile leads you to Community Ditch, crisscrossing another, lower irrigation ditch on the way. Turn right (west) and follow the Community Ditch footpath briefly to the junction of Greenbelt Plateau. After you veer left, this point is the steepest part of the trail—although it's a gentle slope—leading you to the top of Marshall Mesa and a vast prairie. Because of an incredible, unobstructed view, the mountains to the west along the Front Range stand tall and daunting.

Follow the path for about another 1.5 miles, enjoying the scenery, eventually ending at Greenbelt Plateau, 2 miles east of South Broadway on CO 128. Greenbelt Plateau was once a part of the main route from Boulder to Golden.

Marshall Mesa
Trail, Boulder
County Parks and
Open Space

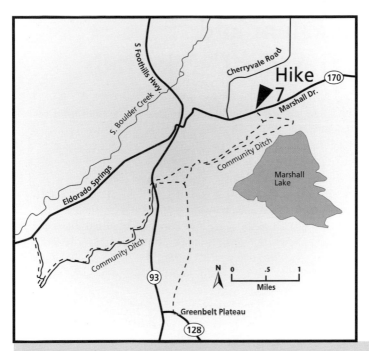

To the trailhead:	The Marshall Mesa Trailhead is on the south side of Marshall Road. Take Broadway (CO 93) south to Marshall Road. Turn left (east) and drive 0.9 mile to the trailhead.
Distance:	4.8 miles round-trip
Difficulty:	Easy
Elevation gain:	350 feet
Dogs:	Yes, on leash
Highlights:	Interpretive signs along the trail denote the historical significance of this former mining town
Jurisdiction:	City of Boulder Open Space & Mountain Parks

The Marshall Mesa to Greenbelt Plateau hike is an easy outing, popular with equestrians and casual folks walking their dogs. It's also an ideal hike for families with young children or school field-trip groups. Be mindful to keep the several gates that you'll pass through closed because of grazing livestock.

Hikers may opt to do a car-swap, parking at both the Greenbelt Plateau and Marshall Mesa Trailheads, cutting the 4.8-mile round-trip excursion to 2.4 miles one-way.

Big Bluestem and South Boulder Creek Trails

Less than 2 miles south of Table Mesa Drive is access to the Big Bluestem and South Boulder Creek trails. The spacious meadow features a diverse landscape and habitat as well as great picnic sites in the shade of a tree.

Combined, the duo makes for an ideal 4.3-mile loop right in the shadow of the Front Range in Boulder. During the winter, given adequate snow pack, these trails offer an exhilarating snowshoe route, gaining just about 300 feet where they merge onto the Mesa Trail (see Hike 25, p. 86).

Starting at the trailhead, begin your hike either on the Big Bluestem Trail, through the gate on the right, or on the South Boulder Creek Trail on the left near the large trailhead sign. Either route is pleasant, straight through spacious pastures, albeit framed with fences and gates to keep intermittent, grazing livestock confined.

South Boulder Creek Trail follows the creek southwest near stands of trees and shrubs. If you've opted to start on this trail first, you'll head uphill a bit along a rocky meadow.

At about 2 miles you'll come to the Mesa Trail junction. The ponderosa pine belt offers shade and a place to stop for lunch. Veer right (west) along the Mesa Trail for a short distance and go right again (north) on the Big Bluestem Trail to begin your descent back to the trailhead.

If you've taken the Big Bluestem Trail from the parking area, obviously you'll reverse that when you get to the Mesa Trail, and loop around veering left (south) to join up with the South Boulder Creek Trail.

If you want to extend your trip by 1.4 miles, continue south after accessing the Mesa Trail, reaching the South Mesa Trailhead at Eldorado Springs Drive. The park has scattered picnic tables and public facilities available.

A range of tempting hiking permutations exists throughout the region. Intersecting along the length of the Mesa Trail is a network of numerous loops that weave through the canyons and ravines. (Avoid bushwhacking and stay on the trail.) The views are nearly unbeatable.

Opposite: East of South Boulder Creek Trail, Boulder County Parks and Open Space

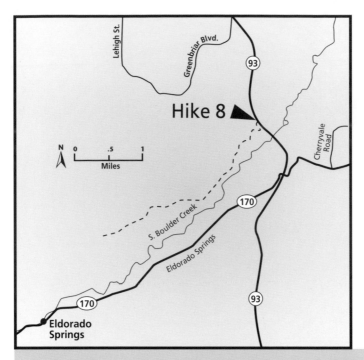

To the trailhead:	South Boulder Creek Trailhead is located 1.9 miles south of Table Mesa Dr. From central Boulder, take Broadway (CO 93) south. Past Table Mesa Dr. Look for Thomas Lane on the right; the trailhead and large parking lot are marked by a Boulder Open Space sign.
Distance:	4.3-mile loop
Difficulty:	Easy
Elevation gain:	About 300 feet
Dogs:	Yes, on leash
Highlights:	A pleasant, scenic loop hike in south Boulder; outhouse at trailhead
Jurisdiction:	City of Boulder Open Space & Mountain Parks

The trails in the area are favorites for runners and hikers and are therefore crowded on weekends. For that reason, if you're seeking solitude, try getting out on a weekday.

Viele Lake

Viele Lake Path,
City of Boulder

Flatlands

Viele Lake, cradled in South Boulder's Harlow Platts Park, sits peacefully against the backdrop of the city's popular flatiron formation. It is here where you'll spot what some consider an abundance of too-tame Canada geese and over-the-top athletic enthusiasts. Each weekend and most weekday evenings, the park bustles with runners and teenagers, retired couples, and people with disabilities, all enjoying the out of doors.

If you're seeking an escape from the Boulder Pearl Street Mall shopping mecca, with its stores, galleries, and restaurants, you'll find it here in a pleasant residential neighborhood. Harlow Platts Park and Viele Lake abut South Boulder Recreation Center at 1360 Gillaspie Drive. The City of Boulder's Parks & Recreation Department offers a variety of skill-building courses at its recreation centers. Classes for kids and adults include sailing, yoga, cooking, instrumental music, golf, pottery, and more.

The park's namesake, Boulder resident Harlow Platts, was a member of the former Parks & Recreation Planning Board for 31 years and a member of the Zoning Board of Adjustment for some 30 years.

The park is one of the few in Boulder that has an extensive Fitness Trail. The cooperative project is sponsored by the City of Boulder Parks and Recreation department, the Boulder Rotary Club, and the Perrier company. Canoes and paddleboats are no longer available for rent at Viele Lake. However, there is still much to see and do in this picturesque recreational area.

The trail itself is wide and concrete, circling the small lake. If you follow the circuit, including the large, arching footbridge, you will have completed a

Crabapple trees, Viele Lake Path, City of Boulder

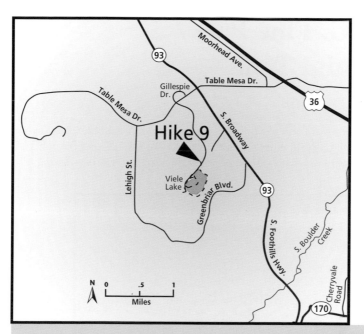

To the trailhead:	Take Broadway (CO 93) south. Turn right (west) on Table Mesa Drive and drive 0.3 mile to Gillaspie Dr. Turn left (south) and follow that street slowly, as you're in a residential district, for 0.8 mile. Parking is on your left.
Distance:	1-mile loop
Difficulty:	Easy
Elevation gain:	Negligible
Dogs:	Yes, on leash
Highlights:	Fitness trail; EXPAND (Exciting Programs, Activities and New Dimensions) for people with disabilities; free public concerts throughout the year, 303-441-3424
Jurisdiction:	City of Boulder Parks and Recreation

1-mile loop skirting the pond. If you only opt to pursue the outside trail, not crossing the bridge, that shortens it to just 0.75 mile.

The creamy stony structure sitting high on a ridge to the east is Boulder Valley School District's Fairview High School.

Eben G. Fine Park / Viewpoint Trail

Named in memory of an early Boulder pharmacist and avid hiker, the Eben G. Fine Park along the Boulder Creek Path (see Hike 1, p. 27) is a pleasant, shady little commons—a good location for picnicking and Frisbee-tossing.

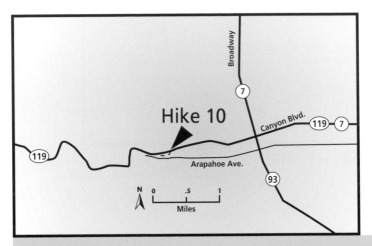

To the trailhead: The park is located near the intersection of 3rd St. and Arapahoe Ave. From Broadway (CO 93), take Arapahoe (CO 7) west.

Distance: 2.4 miles round-trip

Difficulty: Easy to moderate

Elevation gain: 560 feet

Dogs: Yes, on leash or under voice and sight command

Highlights: Charming urban park with access to several trails; public facilities at park

Jurisdiction: City of Boulder Parks and Recreation

Boulder Creek, Eben G. Fine Park, City of Boulder

This is a favorite spot of mine to watch kayakers and canoeists test their prowess in the shallow rapids of Boulder Creek during the spring and summer runoffs. University of Colorado and Boulder High School students also frequent the creek, bracing themselves on their newly purchased inner tubes, riding the cold, cold water all the way down to Broadway.

An appealing short hike, climbing about 560 feet in 1.2 miles, is the Viewpoint Trail. Access to this trail is to the south across Arapahoe Avenue from the Eben G. Fine parking lot.

The footpath winds and climbs southward, with numerous switchbacks, and ends at Panorama Point, about 0.5 mile past the first turn where Baseline Road turns into Flagstaff Road.

Panorama Point offers expansive views of the City of Boulder and further east. Trail connections are plentiful at this south end of the Viewpoint Trail, including routes going further west up Flagstaff Mountain and east toward Chautauqua Park (see Hike 26, p. 89).

This is a good spot to turn around and return the way you came, completing a satisfying 2.4-mile loop.

Back at Eben G. Fine Park, north across Boulder Creek, is Settlers Park (see Hike 11, p. 52). If you prefer to explore those trails, look for the tunnel to the north, at the end of the park with the linkage to the Red Rocks Trail and Settlers Park.

Settlers Park

The Red Rocks Trail leading to large rock fins jutting out of the landscape, that towering pink formation at Settlers Park, is a quiet and peaceful area. The park is a favorite spot of locals because of its proximity to Boulder. Yet precisely because of that, you never really escape the rush and hum of traffic along Canyon Boulevard.

This is the site of dreamy tales of gold, railroads, and Indians. Historians believe Settlers Park got its name because it was the first established, long-term camp of white settlers to the Boulder region. Records indicate that pioneers pitched tents at the base of the rock outcrop nearly 150 years ago in 1858, hoping to strike gold.

To start the hike, walk north from the trailhead on the Pioneer Trail leading to the red rocks. Circle east and around the formation; it's less than 0.5 mile and a meager 300-foot elevation gain.

Here you'll find a trail leading to the easy rock scramble up the formation. Spring is a particularly good time to hike at Settlers Park because of the lovely, vivid assortment of wildflowers in bloom along the irrigation ditches.

Red Rocks "hogback" formation, Settlers Park, City of Boulder

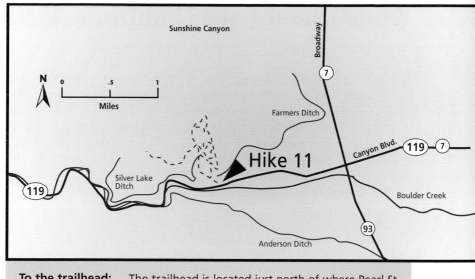

To the trailhead:	The trailhead is located just north of where Pearl St. converges with Canyon Blvd. (CO 7), approximately 1 mile west of Broadway (CO 93).
Distance:	The Settlers Park area is actually a system of short, connecting trails—footpath to the rocky outcrop is about 0.5 mile
Difficulty:	Easy
Elevation gain:	300 feet to the base of Red Rocks
Dogs:	Yes, on leash or under voice and sight command
Highlights:	Towering rock outcrop near the heart of Boulder; popular picnic area for locals
Jurisdiction:	City of Boulder Open Space & Mountain Parks

From Settlers Park you can escape north, down to Sunshine Canyon. Then, you'll reach a connecting trail at Centennial Park to Mount Sanitas (see Hike 36, p. 114). Or, after your Red Rocks ascent, you may opt to continue circling south and head up the short route to Anemone Hill.

The Anemone Hill Trail isn't a loop. Rather, it ends at an aqueduct on what appears to be a former jeep road. The large, snow-covered mountain looming west is Arapaho Peak.

Wonderland Lake/Foothills Trail

Located near the heart of Boulder, with its vibrant downtown area and rich assortment of cultural attractions, Wonderland Lake is the locals' favorite for fishing for both warm- and cold-water species.

For hikers, Wonderland Lake is also an appealing destination. The 2.8-mile Foothills Trail wanders along the north edge of the small lake, extends north to US 36 and is also a good route to take for birding. The wide open views of the plains and foothills frame the lake and dusty footpath.

To the start the short and easy hike, begin at the Foothills Nature Center. Walk from the south side of the building west to the lake, a designated wildlife refuge.

At the northwest end of the lake, head north across the grassland, eventually coming to the Old Kiln Trail on the left. Stay straight and cross Lee Hill Road in about 0.33 mile. Continue walking north and west for about 0.8 mile to another junction. The left fork will take you up a loop along Hogback Ridge (see Hike 13, p. 56), and the right side will lead back down past a prairie dog colony and to the US 36 Foothills Trailhead.

Wonderland Lake, City of Boulder

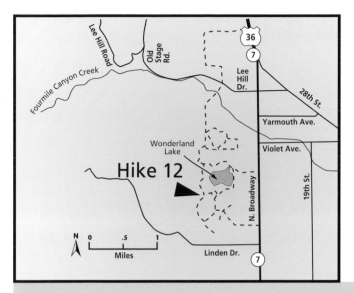

To the trailhead: Access Wonderland Lake and the Foothills Trail at the Foothills Nature Center at 4201 N. Broadway. Take Broadway (CO 93) north to Violet Ave. The trailhead is on an RTD bus route.

Distance: 5.6 miles round-trip

Difficulty: Easy to moderate

Elevation gain: Negligible

Dogs: Yes, on leash

Highlights: Designated wildlife refuge; fishing permitted; Foothills Nature Center, a converted farm house, offers slide shows and nature programs

Jurisdiction: City of Boulder Open Space & Mountain Parks

Before you turn back and return the way you came, look up along the hogback to your left. The Olde Stage Fire of 1990, started by a burning mattress, burned out of control along Hogback Ridge, destroying several residences and nearly reaching US 36. As you hike along the trail, you can see remnants of the devastation and new growth of the vegetation.

The Foothills Trail also connects at its north end to the Boulder Valley Ranch trail system (see Hike 14, p. 58), crossing under the highway to the east and Hogback Ridge to the west.

Hogback Ridge

The fog lifts and dawn sheds a rosy light on Hogback Ridge on a typical summer morning. As it rises in the sky, the sun soon begins to bake the spacious green meadow dotted with colorful wildflowers.

Just north of Boulder, the Hogback Trail loop and Foothills Trail offer visitors a peaceful and picturesque, moderately easy hike.

From the Foothills Trailhead, walk west toward the ridge and under the highway. Continuing west on the Foothills Trail, you'll cross the tiny Silver Lake Ditch. A rather large prairie dog town to the south is filled with the busy, chirping critters. An interpretive sign marks the way.

At about 0.5 mile or so, you'll pass through a gate. Expect a steep climb as you veer left, then take a sharp right near the signs indicating the hookup with the Hogback Loop Trail. At this juncture you may opt to start the loop to the south or north. I generally choose the south (left).

The ridge is a clear shot from here, just meandering along the trail. Expect a marvelous reward at the crest of Hogback Ridge: The shady summit, offering a welcome respite from the exposed and sunny flanks of the knoll.

View to the south, Hogback Trail, Boulder County Parks and Open Space

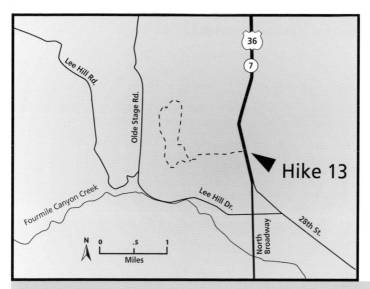

To the trailhead:	The Foothills Trailhead is located about 0.5 mile north of the intersection of US 36 and N. Broadway (CO 7) on the unpaved N. Foothills Hwy. frontage road east of the highway.
Distance:	2.8-mile loop
Difficulty:	Moderate
Elevation gain:	About 900 feet
Dogs:	No
Highlights:	Silent footpath located along a vast prairie of open space lands
Jurisdiction:	City of Boulder Open Space & Mountain Parks

Because the footpath is so narrow, this is a particularly good site for hiking in solitude, allowing time for reflection. And forget the fact that you're unable to see the towering peaks of the Rocky Mountains; it's just a pleasant loop near enough to Boulder and short enough to fit into an otherwise busy day. Because of increasing heat on sunny days and a lack of shade along the route, you may want to pick an early morning to hike up Hogback Ridge during summer months.

Hike 14

Boulder Valley Ranch

About 12 minutes north of downtown Boulder, you can turn off of US 36 and onto the moon. Not exactly, of course, but the expansive monochromatic landscape at Boulder Valley Ranch certainly seems that way.

To the trailhead:	The Boulder Valley Ranch Trailhead is located 1 mile east of US 36 on the south side of Longhorn Road. From central Boulder, take 28th Ave. (US 36) north to Longhorn Road; turn right (east) to the well-marked trailhead.
Distance:	2.5 miles, although many variations and choices are available
Difficulty:	Easy
Elevation gain:	Negligible
Dogs:	Yes
Highlights:	Various trail intersections exist, adding interest to your outing; popular with equestrians; public facilities at trailhead
Jurisdiction:	City of Boulder Open Space & Mountain Parks

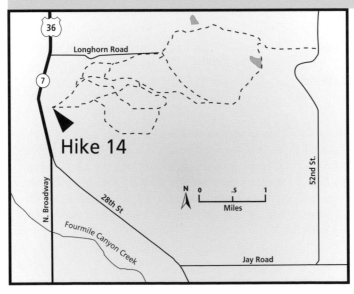

Scattered trees litter the countryside like friendly aliens. Beige and brown hills rise and fall while lazy cows graze and moo. Bikers and hikers, runners, walkers, and equestrians enjoy exploring the miles of interconnecting trails all through the area. Today it is still a working ranch, so hikers and others are asked to keep the gates securely closed when livestock are out grazing.

Short and long, winding and straight trails through this area include the Cobalt and Eagle Trails, Degge and Hidden Valley Trails, and the Sage Trail skirting along Farmers Ditch.

A casual and easy outing includes accessing the Cobalt Trail and walking west for not quite 1 mile, then veering left (east) onto the Eagle Trail for 0.5 mile. You can meander through the desolate, seemingly lunar landscape until you are certain you've gone too far, and then you can opt to go a little further or return the way you came.

Early morning, Mesa Reservoir, Boulder Valley Ranch Open Space

After about 30 minutes or so (depending on your speed), you'll join the Mesa Reservoir Trail for about 1 mile, back to the intersection of Eagle Trail and the Cobalt Trail. The trailhead is about 1 mile east.

Another option from the Boulder Valley Ranch Trailhead is the north segue toward Lefthand Valley Reservoir. From the trailhead, go north about 1.3 miles on the Left Hand Trail all the way to the private reservoir.

Trails etched throughout an otherwise isolated setting, the Boulder Valley Ranch is an ideal place to meditate and bask amongst an otherworldly sense of time and place.

Pella Crossing

This is one of the sites of Colorado's famed ghost towns, located near the present-day town of Hygiene. Few people know that the eastern plains and western canyon lands of Colorado are haunted by some 200 ghost towns, such as the abandoned site of Pella, a one-time bustling thoroughfare between Denver and Laramie. Pella once even maintained a racetrack, school, nursery, and grist mill. Homesteader George Webster (for whom one pond is named) operated an apple orchard at the site.

Back in 1867, the region was unable to endure severe crop losses due to grasshopper infestation. That, combined with residents migrating to larger towns and cities because of railroad and highway accessibility, contributed to the town's demise.

Pella Crossing, named by Hygiene Elementary School students in 1996, designates the center between two historic areas, Pella and North Pella.

The trails at Pella Crossing are pleasant and peaceful, even ethereal, winding around Sunset and Heron Lakes, and Dragonfly, Clearwater, and Poplar Ponds. Boulder County Youth Corps and Wildlands Restoration Volunteers recently helped develop the new area circling Poplar Pond. Anglers, equestrians, and mountain bikers are welcome along the wide, well-marked, crusher-fine pathways.

From the trailhead, choose to go either right along Sunset Lake or left between Webster and Heron Lakes, after a quick review of the trailhead kiosk map. The Braly Trail follows the railroad tracks west of Sunset Lake, and

Last light at Heron Lake, Heron Lake Trail, Pella Crossing

Opposite: Heron Lake Trail, Pella Crossing

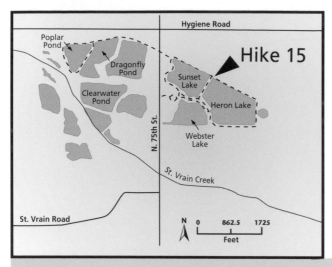

To the trailhead:	Drive north from Boulder on US 36 about 5 miles to Nelson Road. Turn right (east) and proceed 5.9 miles to North 75th Street. Turn left (north). Pella Crossing Open Space will be on your right in about 2 miles. The ample, gravel trailhead is located 1 mile south of the town of Hygiene.
Distance:	Choice of short loops
Difficulty:	Easy
Elevation gain:	Negligible
Dogs:	Yes, on leash
Highlights:	Fishing permitted; non-motorized fishing boats only; a group shelter accommodating up to 50 people available on a first-come, first-serve basis; public facilities and numerous picnic tables available
Jurisdiction:	Boulder County Parks & Open Space

crosses North 75th Street to access the new 1-mile Marlatt Trail around Poplar and Dragonfly Ponds. A plan is underway to extend it south to Clearwater Pond in 2005.

As Marlatt Trail moseys along the edges of the ponds, off in the distance stands a brick steeple of an old country church and some private residences. The Front Range of the Rocky Mountains looms not far to the west. Expect to see dragonflies, waterfowl, red foxes, and maybe even some coyotes, flitting and basking along the shorelines, entertaining watchful visitors.

Coot Lake

The story is that back in the 1970s and early '80s, people used to swim in the nude at tiny Coot Lake just north of Boulder Reservoir. The City of Boulder eventually closed the lake to swimming—and all boating—chiefly because of liability issues. Now the area is inhabited by hikers, runners, and anglers.

Shoreline, Coot Lake, Boulder
County Parks and Open Space

Clouds reflected in Coot Lake, Boulder County Parks and Open Space

A veritable wildlife haven borders the lake, which varies in depth up to only about 20 feet. The great swath of wetlands plays host to the usual variety of waterfowl, including the coots for which the lake is named. Birds of prey also frequent the area because of the nearby prairie dog colony. Many species use the wetlands for breeding and nesting, so visitors are asked to be mindful by not entering designated nesting areas and not allowing dogs to venture off trail.

A visit to Coot Lake is a pleasant outing for families with young children and a nice morning or early-evening walk for anyone seeking a quick and easy getaway close to Boulder.

The hike itself is pretty straightforward, circling the water for just less than 1.5 miles with an offshoot to the south and west toward Boulder Reservoir.

To the trailhead:	From Boulder, take the Diagonal Highway (CO 119) northeast to Longmont. Turn left (north) on 63rd St. Drive about 1 mile to the Coot Lake Trailhead on your left. Parking is limited; additional parking is available across 63rd St. at Tom Watson Park.
Distance:	2.5-mile loop
Difficulty:	Easy
Elevation gain:	Negligible
Dogs:	Yes, on leash
Highlights:	Fishing permitted; prairie dog interpretive trail; public facilities at the trailhead
Jurisdiction:	City of Boulder Open Space & Mountain Parks

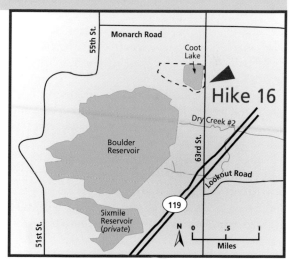

A prairie dog interpretive trail, located 0.33 mile south of Coot Lake, a broad footpath made of crusher-fine gravel, is enhanced by Sue Wise watercolor art combined with conservation and poetry messages. It is designed to encourage appreciation of nature and protection of our environment as well as inform visitors of the richness and diversity of prairie dog habitats. The trail was developed through a grant from the Dr. Scholl Foundation.

The still gray-blue glow of the water reflects the surrounding trees and shrubs like a sheet of glass. The sublime surroundings, offering wide views of the Front Range, allow for a peaceful retreat away from the hustle and bustle of city life.

Walden and Sawhill Ponds

The Sawhill Ponds Wildlife Preserve comprises more than a dozen small lakes. For those of us yearning to hike near water, this is a near-ideal location. A fishing pier is situated out over the larger, shallow lake near the trailhead parking lot.

Canada geese nest during the spring along the wetland area at Sawhill Ponds, along with elusive great horned owls. Amphibians, reptiles, fish, waterfowl, and birds of prey also make their home at Sawhill Ponds.

The Sawhill family owned the land back in the early 1900s and harvested gravel from the ponds for a decade or so. Today, the quiet and peaceful area making up Sawhill Ponds is owned by the Colorado Division of Wildlife and managed by the City of Boulder Open Space & Mountain Parks.

To begin the approximately 2-mile circuit, walk west from the parking area and continue on the wide gravel trail, a former service road built on a dike. As you head west, views of the snowcapped Indian Peaks open up along the horizon. Continue on, passing four tiny lakes on your right and one larger lake to your left.

After passing those, veer right (north) and continue. Soon you'll have the option to take another right and head back east or continue north, opting for another right-hand fork later. You can't get lost if you remember to walk east when you want to return to your car. And it's refreshing to just meander along and enjoy the marshy wetlands with its network of trails and bouquets of cattails jutting out of the waters.

This isn't the place to go if you're seeking a strenuous workout with some serious elevation gain, although I've seen several visitors run the trails for a higher-intensity exercise experience.

Sunrise at Sawhill Ponds, Boulder County Parks and Open Space

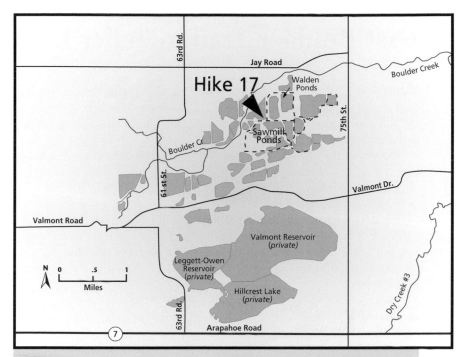

To the trailhead: The trailhead is on the west side of 75th St., between Valmont and Jay Roads. Take 75th St. to just north of the railroad tracks, north of Valmont Road. Turn left (west). An RTD bus route is nearby.

Distance: 2-mile loop

Difficulty: Easy

Elevation gain: Negligible

Dogs: Yes, on leash

Highlights: Fishing permitted; picnic tables and benches scattered throughout the area; public facilities at the trailhead

Jurisdiction: City of Boulder Open Space & Mountain Parks manages Sawhill Ponds for the Colorado Division of Wildlife; the Walden Ponds Wildlife Habitat is managed by Boulder County Parks and Open Space

A walk north will get you to the Walden Ponds composite of lakes, marshes, brush and cottonwoods. Pelican Marsh, the largest pond, was created by gravel mining, which was completed in 1998.

East Boulder Trail to Teller Lake

Whether you hike, bike, or ride horseback, an outing along the East Boulder Trail north through the Teller Farm area is sure to satisfy your yearning for the outdoors. The route is popular with equestrians and trail runners, and is entirely wheelchair accessible.

Named for the late Senator Henry Teller, who worked the extensive acreage, the privately owned working farmland abutting the trail is used for cattle and horse grazing, crop production, and bee keeping. Several small lakes, all named Teller, dot the area.

To start the hike, access the trailhead from the south end, east of 75th Street off of Arapahoe Road. Walking east for a short distance, you'll soon pass one of the Teller Lakes with its fishing pier. Because the Teller Lakes are designated wildlife preserves, dogs must stay on leash when within 100 yards of the water.

Next, veer north (left) and continue along the smooth and level trail, a decades-old gravel service road. The City of Boulder has negotiated a conservation easement, thus all travel is restricted to designated trails.

East Boulder Trail to Teller Lakes

To the trailhead:	The East Boulder Trail–Teller Lake Trailhead is located 1 mile east of 75th St. on Arapahoe Road. Turn left (north) off of Arapahoe and drive 0.6 mile to the trailhead parking area.
Distance:	About 6.5 miles one-way
Difficulty:	Easy to moderate, depending upon distance
Elevation gain:	300 feet
Dogs:	Yes, on leash or under voice and sight command; on leash only within 100 yards of water. No dogs are allowed along the White Rocks Preserve section of the East Boulder Trail.
Highlights:	Fishing permitted; wheelchair accessible; large parking area with public facilities and picnic tables
Jurisdiction:	City of Boulder Open Space & Mountain Parks

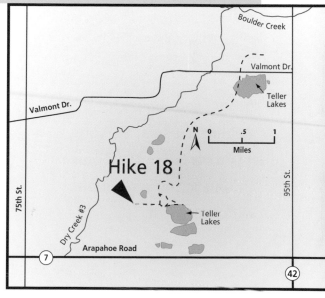

As the trail winds north, framed by large cottonwood trees, views all along the Front Range span to the east and west, north and south. You'll pass Dry Creek Davidson Ditch, Leyner Cottonwood Ditch, and one of the larger Teller Lakes before you cross Valmont Drive in 2.2 miles.

After crossing Valmont Drive, continue north to enter the White Rocks Nature Preserve, with wetlands to your left (west) and a small stream to the right of the trail. Dogs are not allowed north of Valmont Drive.

After crossing a bridge and Leggett Ditch, the footpath takes a sharp left (west) turn, offering some gradual ups and downs, eventually ending at Boulderado and Cambridge streets in the Heatherwood neighborhood of Gunbarrel.

Turn back and return the way you came. Savvy visitors who've planned ahead may have scheduled a car swap at each end of the lengthy trail.

Foothills

Where the plains, or flatlands, rise to meet the mountains is dubbed the foothills. For hundreds of miles, at an approximate elevation of between 5,500 to 8,000 feet, the Rocky Mountain foothills spread the length of Colorado from Wyoming to New Mexico. And just as urban sprawl is edging eastward along the Front Range, it is also melding into the foothills to the west.

The wooded slopes of our nearby foothills attract crowd-weary residents of Boulder, Longmont, Denver, and points beyond. This lower montane zone supports stands of ponderosa pine and Douglas fir. Deer, bobcats, lizards, sage grouse, prairie dogs, and chipmunks may be spotted in the forests and valleys.

There's much allure to hiking on these peaceful, often shaded and not-so-shaded roads and trails. However, the reality is that the trails are easily accessed by hundreds of people, thus requiring an attention to balance between wilderness and civilization. Be mindful not to take your city ways into the hills: Walk quietly and speak softly.

> **"Now I see the secret of making the best persons, it is to grow in the open air and to eat and sleep with the earth."**
>
> **—Walt Whitman**

Many of the following hikes located in the foothills wander through the shadows of the towering, craggy mountains that frame Boulder so spectacularly. The hikes, while varying in difficulty, terrain, and views, all have one thing in common: A link to the busy, urban landscape of the flatlands to the east and the real and rugged world of the mountains to the west.

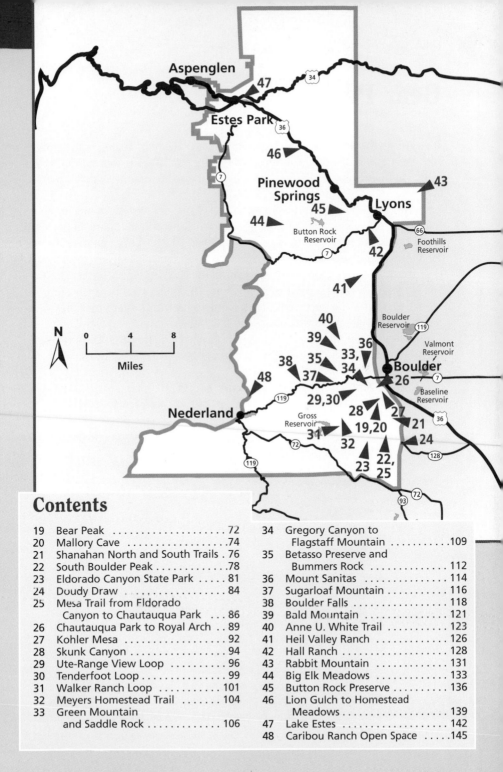

Contents

Bear Peak

If you're at all wondering what local hike will offer the most lasting impression, Bear Peak may be the one. This tough trail leading to its 8,461-foot summit will leave you huffing and puffing yet awestruck at the surrounding beauty from the very top.

With its pointed profile, Bear Peak is one of Boulder's most prominent mountains. The steep and seemingly unrelenting Fern Canyon Trail leading to Bear Peak is strenuous, but so satisfying when accomplished. The fern-filled gulch and peaceful, forested footpath offers solitude as well as an athletic challenge.

This hike is accessible nearly any time of the year. If you venture out during the early fall weeks, raspberries ripen along the upper trail near the summit, attracting bears and hikers alike. I once spotted a big brown bear munching some sweet berries in the bushes alongside the trail. All bears warrant a wide berth.

To begin, from the National Center for Atmospheric Research (NCAR) take the Walter Orr Roberts Trail west to the Dakota Trail, walking along a small mesa leading down to a broad saddle.

Climb a gently sloping ridge to a water tank before hiking into the valley and joining the Mesa Trail (see Hike 25, p. 86), turning left (south). If you

Bear Peak and fall foliage, Bear Creek Trail, City of Boulder Open Space & Mountain Parks

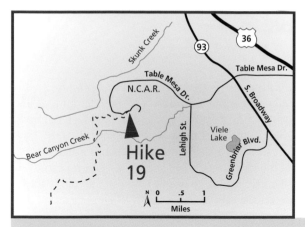

To the trailhead:	Drive west on Table Mesa Dr. 2 miles past the intersection with Broadway (CO 93). Park at the north lot of the National Center for Atmospheric Research (NCAR) and access the Walter Orr Roberts Trail.
Distance:	5.6 miles round-trip
Difficulty:	Strenuous
Elevation gain:	2,381 feet
Dogs:	Yes, on leash
Highlights:	Spectacular views from summit; rugged and rocky hike along the way
Jurisdiction:	City of Boulder Open Space & Mountain Parks

choose to go right, the route is less steep but you will extend the length of the hike by about 1.5 miles.

Going left takes you into Fern Canyon, with its sheer rock faces rising straight up in some areas. This trail forks off of the Mesa Trail. Walk southward, then go right (west) to begin a brutal, rock-stepping climb. In the warmer months, the narrow trail pushes through thick ferns, tall grasses, and a variety of berry shrubs rising to the summit of Bear Peak.

About two-thirds of the way up is a spacious saddle—a well-deserved resting area. From here you can make your ascent up Bear Peak. If you're feeling ambitious, from the saddle you can also access South Boulder Peak, about 0.75 mile to the left (southwest). (See Hike 22, p. 78)

If you reach the summit during the late afternoon, expect predictable, gusty winds, and take the necessary precautions.

Mallory Cave

If you like caves, this one is dark and mysterious, shallow and spacious.

Mallory Cave is Boulder's great not-so-hidden cavern. Beginning at an elevation of approximately 6,080 feet and ending at about 7,020 feet, the trail leading to Mallory Cave is one of the most rewarding in Boulder County. The entrance to the cave, situated deep in a cleft among sandstone formations, offers hikers great views of Boulder, Denver, and the entire eastern plains.

During the summer months, bats sleep upside down on the roof of the cave throughout the day. To protect the bats while they nest, Mallory Cave and the adjacent slopes are closed from April 1 to October 1.

In 1932, an 18-year-old named E. C. Mallory came upon the cave that had been previously found, but never recorded, by two Boulder-area lumberjacks.

The Mallory Cave Trail wanders through ponderosa pine and fir trees along the eastern flanks of Dinosaur Mountain. An attractive trail, it increases in steepness with a snaking queue of switchbacks.

Bear Peak and sculptured sandstone, Walter Orr Roberts Trail, NCAR Mesa

To the trailhead:	Mallory Cave is located between Eldorado Springs and Chautauqua Park. Drive west on Table Mesa Dr. 2 miles past the intersection with Broadway (CO 93). Park at the north lot of NCAR and access the Walter Orr Roberts Trail.
Distance:	2.2 miles round-trip
Difficulty:	Moderate with some steep grades; access to the cave requires a scramble up a rock chute
Elevation gain:	940 feet
Dogs:	Yes, on leash
Highlights:	Seasonal closures while bats nest; good hike for youngsters
Jurisdiction:	City of Boulder Open Space & Mountain Parks

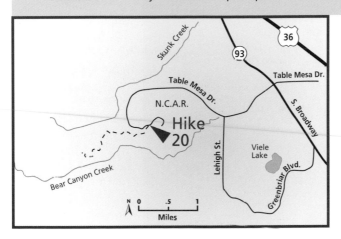

The hike starts at the Walter Orr Roberts Trail, just west of the National Center for Atmospheric Research (NCAR) facilities. Follow the footpath to the Dakota Trail, crossing over the Dakota Formation, to a water tank marking the Mesa Trail (see Hike 25, p. 86).

Heading left (south) on the Mesa Trail, you will soon spot the sign pointing to Mallory Cave. Climb to a large rock outcrop, and go around its southern face. Then proceed up and behind to the north.

The last several hundred feet or so present a stepping-stone challenge between chunks of pink sandstone. Entering the cave requires a moderate 50-foot climb up a sandstone slab—the most exciting part of the hike to youngsters. Scramble up the rock notch and over some steep rock walls. This final pitch is nothing technical. All it takes is a firm determination to enter Mallory Cave.

Shanahan North and South Trails

If you are finding yourself marooned too often on the couch in front of the television with a bag of chips, guacamole, and soda, feeling like you could definitely use some exercise, then you're in luck: The Shanahan North and South Trails present a formidable workout loop. The 4.3-mile ring isn't too strenuous and offers up a good approximation of secluded wilderness in south Boulder.

Ponderosa pines, South Shanahan Ridge Trail, Boulder County Parks and Open Space

To begin the hike, locate the marked trailhead in a residential neighborhood. Take this rocky footpath to a junction marked with a wooden kiosk and turn right (north). Proceed up an incline toward the North Fork Shanahan Trail. You will eventually turn left (west) onto the North Fork Shanahan Trail and meet up with the Mesa Trail (see Hike 25, p. 86) in about 1.5 miles. If you continued along the North Fork Shanahan Trail, you would end at the Fern Canyon Trail (see Hike 19, p. 72). However, save this outing for another day.

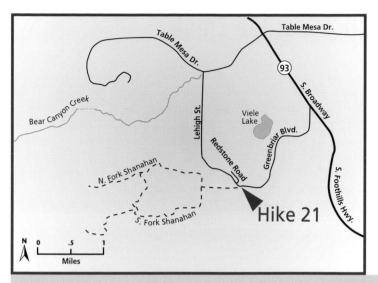

To the trailhead:	Take S. Broadway (CO 93) south to Greenbriar Ave. Turn right (west) past Fairview High School and drive about 1 mile, parking near the intersection of Lehigh St. and Redstone Road. Be mindful where you park in this residential neighborhood.
Distance:	4.3-mile loop
Difficulty:	Easy to moderate
Elevation gain:	820 feet
Dogs:	Yes, on leash or under voice and sight command
Highlights:	Pleasant loop hike in a forested area; connections to other trail systems
Jurisdiction:	Boulder County Parks and Open Space

As you continue, turn left (south) along the Mesa Trail for just about 0.5 mile to the South Fork Shanahan Trail, then turn left (east), creating a loop. Follow this gravel road, and the return trip to the trailhead is entirely downhill. You will come to a meadow in about 0.7 mile and the trail will narrow. Follow the trail through the forest for 0.5 mile to another gravel road. At this area, go back to your first intersection with the trail map marker. Return home and resume snacking in front of the television—or not.

Foothills

South Boulder Peak

Because South Boulder Peak lies west of Bear Peak (see Hike 19, p. 72), it isn't seen from most vantage points in Boulder. Nevertheless, the views from its summit are magnificent. This is a mountain summit you'll remember.

The Shadow Canyon route gains roughly 3,000 vertical feet, winding steeply up and through forests scattered with boulders, ultimately rewarding hikers with exhilarating vistas. It's a well-traveled trail for athletic Boulderites as well as those of us who aren't particularly athletic.

To begin the hike, access the South Mesa Trailhead. After crossing a large wooden footbridge, you'll soon join the Homestead or Towhee Trail—it doesn't matter which you choose, as both routes eventually merge with the South Mesa Trail entering Shadow Canyon.

On your way up, you'll pass two primitive cabins. The first one on your left is the McGillivary Cabin, a quintessential homestead structure built in the late 1800s. The second cabin bordering the small creek, the Stockton Cabin, was probably built as a miner's lodge in the late 1800s as well. It is now called the Stockton Cabin for Roscoe Stockton, a writer and teacher who purchased the lodge and surrounding land in 1910.

After you've passed the Stockton Cabin on the right side of the trail near the mouth of the canyon, you'll begin a pretty brutal climb. Consider the scenic beauty and enjoy the fragrant forest scent while you're huffing and puffing.

Rock formations, Towhee Trail, Bear Peak, City of Boulder Open Space & Mountain Parks

Opposite: Shadow Canyon between South Boulder Peak and Bear Peak, City of Boulder Open Space & Mountain Parks

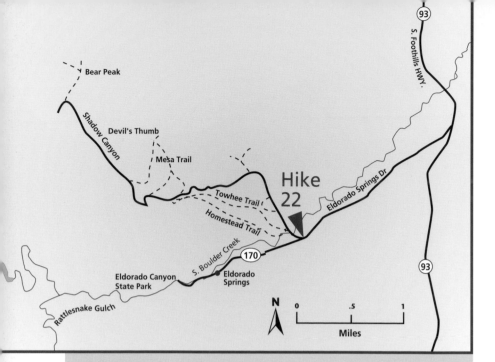

To the trailhead:	Take Broadway (CO 93) south to the stoplight at Eldorado Springs Dr. Turn right (west) and drive for about 1.7 miles to the Mesa Trailhead. Parking is on the north and south sides of the street.
Distance:	About 5.8 miles round-trip
Difficulty:	Strenuous
Elevation gain:	2,779 feet
Dogs:	Yes, on leash
Highlights:	Rock-strewn summit offers 360-degree views of the Front Range and beyond; public facilities at trailhead
Jurisdiction:	City of Boulder Open Space & Mountain Parks

The trail will gain a steep 1,600 feet in about 1 mile. Continue on this unrelenting yet pleasingly wooded area, and you will reach a spacious saddle separating Bear and South Boulder Peaks.

South Boulder Peak, your destination, is to the left (southwest) while Bear Peak is to the right (north). Both involve another 20 minutes or so of manageable rock climbing (nothing technical). From the South Boulder Peak summit, Gross Reservoir and Walker Ranch lie below and the views of Longs Peak and Pikes Peak dominate the landscape further beyond.

Eldorado Canyon State Park

The Bastille and Shirt Tail Peak, Fowler
Trail, Eldorado Canyon State Park

Foothills

It would be genuinely difficult to find a more appealing family park than Eldorado Canyon State Park, with its more than 12 miles of rugged and well-worn trails. On a hot summer day, it's particularly satisfying to trek the 3.5 miles along Eldorado Canyon Trail, ending at South Boulder Creek, where you can sit and soak your feet in the chilly water.

The beauty of this area is that it offers a refurbished and upscale Visitors Center, an abundance of picnic tables, and a sideshow of seemingly fearless rock climbers often seen scaling the nearby cliffs. World-renowned for its more than 500 technical rock climbing routes and the famous Eldorado Springs Resort (established near the turn of the 20th century), the area also features spacious, open meadows and forested hills for hikers to enjoy.

To begin the hike, go north from the Visitors Center and climb some narrow steps. The route ultimately ascends more than 1,000 vertical feet with sharp, but not difficult, switchbacks.

About 20 minutes into the hike you'll reach a small saddle. Follow the clearly identifiable trail, crossing a forested gully onto the west-facing draw. Looking south and up, you can see the Denver and Rio Grande railroad grade along what appears to be a precipitous canyon wall. You'll also spot a recently

painted bright red private residence along the hillside.

The Continental Divide to the west is generally sprinkled with a sheer, soft blanket of snow well into July. Fragrant pine trees and incredible views all along the path remind us why we love Colorado. Be sure to bring a camera. On hot, sunny days the trail is dry and dusty. You can get fairly thirsty, so bring plenty of water, too.

Continuing on, expect to ascend and descend about 10 more switchbacks, reaching the western edge of the meadow. From here you'll

Eldorado Canyon, Rattlesnake Gulch Trail, Eldorado Canyon State Park

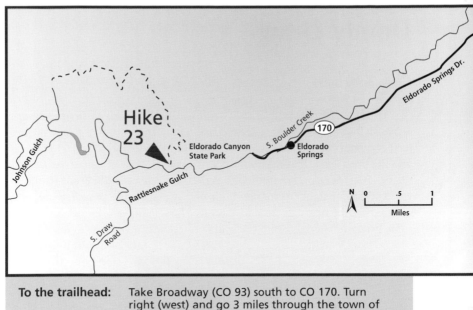

To the trailhead:	Take Broadway (CO 93) south to CO 170. Turn right (west) and go 3 miles through the town of Eldorado Springs, entering Eldorado Canyon State Park. There is an entrance fee per vehicle. Follow the signs and park at the Visitors Center lot.
Distance:	Approximately 7 miles round-trip; 10-mile loop possible
Difficulty:	Moderately strenuous
Elevation gain:	1,040 feet
Dogs:	Yes, on leash
Highlights:	Visitors Center, picnic tables; world-renowned rock climbing area
Jurisdiction:	Colorado State Parks

climb down steeply to the canyon floor, listening to the rush of South Boulder Creek guiding you.

Once at South Boulder Creek, you may opt to extend your hike on the Eldorado Canyon Trail to connect with the Columbine Gulch Trail, South Boulder Creek Trail, and the Crescent Meadows Trail, completing a 10-mile loop. Or you can turn around and return the way you came.

The Fowler Trail (not quite 1 mile and fairly level) and Rattlesnake Gulch Trail (1.9 miles gaining 1,020 vertical feet) are optional routes also accessible from the park, south of the creek.

Foothills

Doudy Draw

Cattle graze the tableland and the views west, north, and south are seemingly endless along the Doudy Draw Open Space.

The Doudy Draw Trail, with its connecting Flatirons Vista Trailhead, draws visitors to the heart of open space lands. This round-trip trek pushes the parameters of an easy hike, but it does so in invigorating ways, taking you into the open space that makes Boulder so special. Hikers, equestrians, Nordic skiers, and others are rewarded with remarkable views of the Front Range.

The Junior Ranger Program built part of the Doudy Draw Trail in 1986 with assistance from the Boulder County Horseman Association. Although some printed materials claim the trail is wheelchair accessible, in reality, parts of the trail further along into the hike don't appear to be particularly wheelchair-friendly.

Foothills, Dowdy Draw Trail, Boulder County Parks and Open Space

Begin your outing from the Flatirons Vista Trailhead adjacent to the horse corrals. The first part of the trail heading west is a bumpy little sector with strewn rocks, but after about 100 yards the path levels out.

The initial half of this well-marked footpath follows electrical poles and you will pass through a number of gates that keep the intermittent grazing livestock from escaping. Climb a brief ascent leading to the top of the mesa along an exposed meadow with scattered ponderosa pine trees. Continue on the footpath, opening and closing several gates.

Walking along the grassy plateau will lead you into a forest along a ridge overlooking the draw. Climb along the ridge—which isn't dangerous at all—until you begin your climb downward into the valley below. Right about here you may want to get out a camera, although the panoramic views all along this area aptly reflect its name: Flatirons Vista.

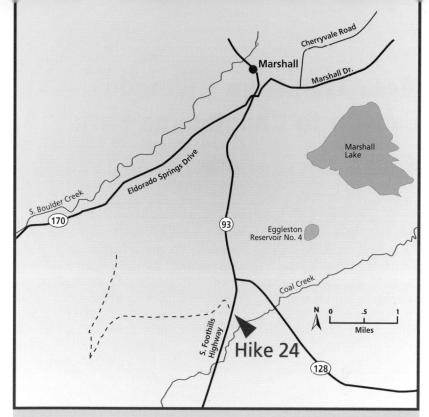

To the trailhead:	The Flatirons Vista Trailhead is located on the right side (west) of Broadway (CO 93), 2 miles south of its intersection with Eldorado Springs Dr. (CO 170). Take Broadway south through the town of Marshall and past the intersection with CO 128.
Distance:	6.6 miles round-trip
Difficulty:	Easy
Elevation gain:	Gain and loss of approximately 540 feet
Dogs:	Yes, on leash or under voice and sight control. Because of the possible presence of black bears, it is recommended that dogs be on leash on the upper portion of the Doudy Draw Trail.
Highlights:	Suitable for snowshoeing and cross-country skiing given adequate snow; ample parking available
Jurisdiction:	City of Boulder Open Space & Mountain Parks

Making a sharp switchback, continue the final 1.5 miles or so into the valley north along a stream, crossing Community Ditch and ending at the Doudy Draw Trailhead, 2 miles west of Broadway on Eldorado Springs Drive.

Mesa Trail from Eldorado Canyon to Chautauqua Park

Achieving an elevation gain of 1,400 vertical feet along the Mesa Trail from south to north, hikers begin and end at about the same elevation—5,600 feet to 5,680 feet.

Stretching 6.1 miles from Eldorado Canyon (see Hike 23, p. 81) to Chautauqua Park (see Hike 26, p. 89), this is a long hike. Even though there is no significant elevation change from its southern starting point to its northern end at Boulder's popular Chautauqua Park, the trail climbs and drops again and again along its length, adding interest to the hike. And depending on your intensity, the hike provides a good aerobic workout as well.

Starting from the trailhead, access the south end of the Mesa Trail by walking north and crossing a bridge over South Boulder Creek. Be sure not to veer left: That would take you straight up into Shadow Canyon (see Hike 22, p. 78). Near here, on your left, is the historic stone Doudy-Debacker-Dunn House.

Be sure to walk directly north, following a wide left turn on the trail westward, only after you've passed the turnoff leading into Shadow Canyon.

Walking the length of the Mesa Trail, you'll see offshoots leading to Fern, Bear, and Gregory Canyons (see Hike 34, p. 109), and Green Mountain (see Hike 33, p. 106). Spacious meadows and excellent views of the Flatirons and Devil's Thumb reward hikers as well.

The trail will briefly become the Big Bluestem Trail (see Hike 8, p. 44) if you veer further to the east, still heading north and a bit westward. Don't fret if you find yourself on this trail, as it hooks up with the Mesa Trail on your way further north.

You'll detour off the well-worn Mesa Trail if you take a hard left or right turn, so simply follow the footpath north across the mesas. Halfway into the hike is a radio tower, at an elevation of about 6,400 feet. From here, it's downhill all the way, dumping into gorgeous Chautauqua Park.

You'll pass segues east to the Skunk Canyon Trail (see Hike 28, p. 94), and a west spur to Woods Quarry before actually entering the charming and historic Chautauqua Park.

Because of the length of the trail, runners and hikers may opt to do a car swap at each end of the trail.

Mesa Trail and Flatirons from
McClintock Trail

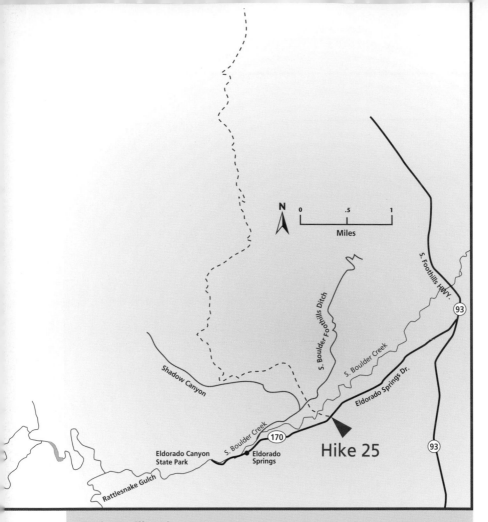

To the trailhead: Take Broadway (CO 93) south to the stoplight at Eldorado Springs Dr. (CO 170). Turn right (west) for about 1.5 miles to the marked trailhead. Parking is on the north and south sides of the street.

Distance: 6.1 miles one-way

Difficulty: Moderate

Elevation gain: 1,000 feet gain and loss

Dogs: Yes, on leash or under voice and sight command

Highlights: Picnic tables; ample parking; accesses other trail connections

Jurisdiction: Colorado State Parks (Eldorado Canyon side); City of Boulder Open Space & Mountain Parks (Chautauqua Park north end)

Chautauqua Park to Royal Arch

As far back as 1898, Boulder residents recognized the value of preserving open lands and purchased picturesque Chautauqua Park as a mountain backdrop. The first trail leading to the Royal Arch was built soon after. However, it wasn't until about 1921 that the present trail leading to the Arch was built by some ambitious Boy Scouts, Ernest M. Greenman, Eben G. Fine, and the Boulder Rotarians.

This area, with its historic auditorium, quaint dining hall, and tiny cottages, is home to a number of looping and intersecting trails, leading into the foothills. Accessible trails from this starting point include the McClintock (0.7 mile) and Enchanted Mesa (1.2 miles) trails. Woods Quarry, at just 0.3 mile, starts at the north end of the Mesa Trail (See Hike 25, p. 86) and ends at an abandoned quarry. Other trails at the park include the Kohler Mesa (1 mile, see Hike 27, p. 92), Bluebell Mesa (0.6 mile), and Bluebell-Baird (0.7 mile) trails.

Chautauqua Meadow, Chautauqua Park, City of Boulder Open Space & Mountain Parks

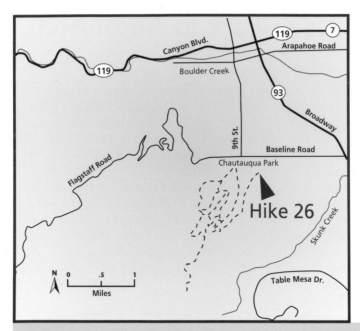

To the trailhead: Chautauqua Park is located on the south side of Baseline Road near 9th St., west of Broadway (CO 93). Parking is always a challenge, so visitors are advised to arrive early, even on a weekday morning.

Distance: 3 miles round-trip

Difficulty: Somewhat strenuous

Elevation gain: 1,270 feet

Dogs: Yes, on leash

Highlights: Picnic tables; shelter; ranger information cabin; historic auditorium; arch represents a fabulous geological oddity

Jurisdiction: City of Boulder Open Space & Mountain Parks

You can also access the Saddle Rock (1.3 miles), E.M. Greenman (1.4 miles), and Ranger (1.1 miles) trails leading to the 8,144-foot summit of Green Mountain (see Hike 33, p. 106).

The quick climb up to the Royal Arch starts at Chautauqua Park. This stunning sandstone formation that looms over southwest Boulder rises at

the conclusion of what seems like a long, brutal, hilly, and exhausting trail. You'll gain 1,270-feet in about 1.5 miles, crossing over a couple of wooden bridges and passing through forests, meadows, and a large boulder field. Oh, but the rewards of reaching the spectacular Royal Arch are worth every step.

Royal Arch seen from the south side, City of Boulder Open Space & Mountain Parks

To begin the short hike, from the Chautauqua parking lot, walk southwest through Chautauqua Meadows on a fairly steep incline, veering left onto Bluebell Baird Trail. You'll soon come upon a few picnic tables and the Bluebell Shelter.

Go right following the sign indicating the Arch Trail and continue through a shaded ponderosa pine forest. The trail goes into Bluebell Canyon, offering a series of switchbacks to gain a ridge. Reaching a saddle named Sentinel Pass, you can enjoy views of the south face of the Third Flatiron.

From the saddle, you'll climb down steeply onto the outer side of the ridge. Follow the trail climbing past Tangen Spring, then make a steep ascent for a short distance to end at the Royal Arch. Step through the Arch and view a vast sea of red-tiled roofs of the University of Colorado to the northeast. Watch your footing as you sit on a large rock to enjoy magnificent views of the entire southeast Boulder Valley.

Either before or after you've tackled the Royal Arch hike, be sure to swing by the ranger's cabin near the parking area and pick up maps and information about the other trails originating from Chautauqua Park.

Foothills

Kohler Mesa

Hiking is rarely ordinary, even if only 30 minutes or so from home. Such is the case with an excursion along the Four Pines Trail, hooking up along Kohler Mesa in the foothills. Expect the unexpected and look forward to having a great, albeit short, hike. The trail is well-maintained, accessible year-round, and a map at the trailhead will familiarize you with the route.

Access the Four Pines Trail, going right (west) at the trailhead and climbing a small hill past a rest area with a poignant memorial marker. You'll gain some 300 feet or so.

Continue into the foothills past an antenna field. There are two trails: a dirt road on your left and a footpath on your right, both leading to a broad mesa. The trails merge again further up at a fence.

Four Pines Trail, Kohler Mesa, City of Boulder Open Space & Mountain Parks

To the trailhead:	From Broadway (CO 93), drive west on Baseline Road to 17th St. Turn left (south) and proceed four blocks to the Four Pines Trailhead parking area on your left.
Distance:	About 2.5 miles round-trip
Difficulty:	Easy
Elevation gain:	704 feet
Dogs:	Yes, on leash
Highlights:	Convenient, short hike in the heart of Boulder
Jurisdiction:	City of Boulder Open Space & Mountain Parks

You'll keep going southwest, bearing left at a fork, then right at another fork along the trail. The trail connects with the Mesa Trail (see Hike 25, p. 86), but you may opt to turn around here and return the way you came, making a formidable 2.4 mile round-trip with an elevation gain of 704 feet.

It's a pleasant outing, particularly on a clear summer or fall evening. This is also an ideal hike to do with children.

Skunk Canyon

A short hike along south Boulder's Skunk Canyon, with its slender grasses, rock-strewn footpath, and perhaps (if you're lucky) sight of a timid neighborhood deer, will lure you back again and again. The trail echoes of pioneer beginnings and voices of nature. The Skunk Canyon Trail remains a nature setting, and is an important trail corridor connecting to other routes that penetrate the forested areas further west.

To the trailhead:	To access the trail at the corner of Vassar and Table Mesa Drives, from Broadway (CO 93) drive west on Table Mesa Dr. past Bear Creek Elementary to Vassar Dr. on your right. Park with discretion on the street in this quiet neighborhood.
Distance:	2.6 miles round-trip
Difficulty:	Easy
Elevation gain:	550 feet
Dogs:	Yes, on leash or under voice and sight command
Highlights:	Nice introductory hike for children and older adults
Jurisdiction:	City of Boulder Open Space & Mountain Parks

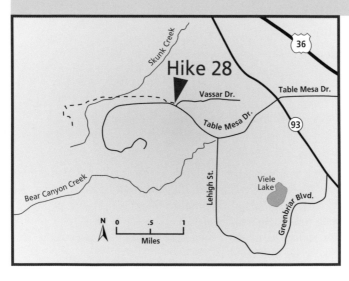

Access the trailhead at the corner of Table Mesa and Vassar Drives in south Boulder, being courteous as you're parking in a neighborhood. Walk west along an old fire road only about 0.5 mile into the open space. You'll be walking on a wide, paved section for a while.

Cross Skunk Creek on a small wooden bridge and continue west along a sustained, gradual ascent. As you follow the dirt road, you'll pass by an electrical substation on your left and the backyards of residences to your right. The trail eventually narrows and is framed by an interesting variety of assorted shrubs and bushes, but no aspen trees.

Essentially, this short trail is a nature walk through a metropolitan wilderness. As you make your way, a junction to Kohler Mesa (see Hike 27, p. 92) is on your right. Continuing to climb, you'll pass by a boulder field of large pink and gray stones to the right and left of the footpath, with the Mesa Trail (see Hike 25, p. 86) above you.

The route contours across two gullies, connecting to the Mesa Trail in a meadow in about 0.8 mile or 20 minutes, depending, of course, on your pace.

This is a very pleasant, not-too-strenuous hike, suitable as an after-dinner outing or invigorating early morning pick-me-up.

Ute-Range View Loop

The dusty and rugged trails on Flagstaff Mountain offer some of the best local hiking available, and the Ute-Range View Loop is no exception.

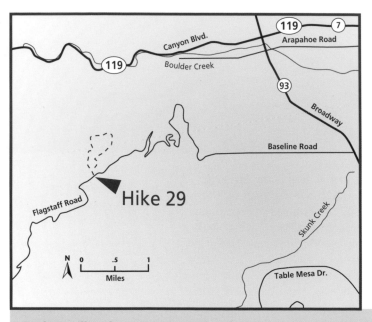

To the trailhead:	From Chautauqua Park, take Baseline Road west (it will merge into Flagstaff Road). Drive 3.3 miles and park at Realization Point. The trailhead is to the east of the parking areas. Parking fees are charged for vehicles not registered in Boulder County.
Distance:	1-mile loop
Difficulty:	Easy
Elevation gain:	140 feet
Dogs:	Yes, under sight and voice command or on leash
Highlights:	Picnic shelters, interpretive markers; great route for young children
Jurisdiction:	City of Boulder Open Space & Mountain Parks

Forest fog, Ute-Range View Trail,
Flagstaff Mountain

Foothills

The Range View Trail begins near Realization Point, curving east along Flagstaff Mountain through forested meadows traveled by a variety of wildlife: mule deer, foxes, coyotes, and raptors. I spotted nearly a dozen deer sitting in the shade atop Flagstaff Mountain one afternoon. I was pleased they didn't appear spooked as I quietly walked past them on the trail.

After you've accessed the footpath at Realization Point, expect four switchbacks along a glacial boulder field. Because of the ease of the hike, this route is ideally suited for families with small children and even classrooms of young students. Numerous interpretive signs dot the trails throughout the area.

You'll come upon a chunky staircase made of boulders. Behind you, the Indian Peaks rise to the west. Looking north, the forested mountains reach skyward as if gently blanketed onto the landscape.

From the north end of the Range View Trail you can take the fork left (west) to join the Boy Scout Trail for not quite 1 mile to Mays Point, accessing a scenic overlook. This segue, however worthwhile, would add 2 miles to your hike (out and back).

If you opt not to go to the overlook, take the right fork and follow the path as it curves gradually south, hooking up with the Ute Trail. Continue heading south rather than eastward toward the picnic shelters. The 0.5-mile Ute Trail provides views of the plains flowing endlessly toward Denver and beyond as it returns to Realization Point.

Green Mountain, seen from Gregory Canyon

Tenderfoot Loop

There was a lovely mantle of clouds sort of hovering above the top of the mountains to the west on the day I hiked the Tenderfoot Loop on Flagstaff Mountain. The short and tidy trails looping and intersecting atop Flagstaff Mountain offer impressive hiking routes, further contributing to why so many of us choose to hike here.

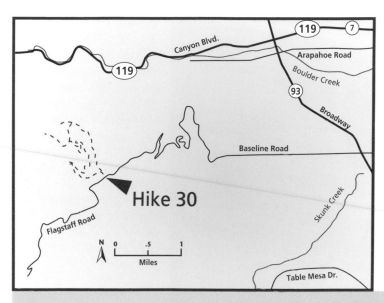

To the trailhead:	From Chautauqua Park, take Baseline Road west (it will merge into Flagstaff Road). Drive 3.3 miles and park at Realization Point. The trailhead is to the east of the parking areas. Parking fees are charged for vehicles not registered in Boulder County.
Distance:	2.5-mile loop
Difficulty:	Easy to moderate
Elevation gain:	500 feet
Dogs:	Yes, under sight and voice command or on leash
Highlights:	Large trailhead kiosk; up-front and close views of the Front Range and Sugarloaf Mountain
Jurisdiction:	City of Boulder Open Space & Mountain Parks

The Tenderfoot Trail is a pleasant, moderately tough (in a good way) 2.5-mile loop curving and zigzagging along the flanks of Flagstaff Mountain. The fragrant coniferous forest is inhabited by a variety of animals and birds, and in areas offers outstanding views of the Indian Peaks to the west.

After parking at Realization Point, locate the Tenderfoot Trailhead sign. Take the Chapman fire road downhill through a ponderosa pine and fir forest.

About 10 minutes into the hike, past the cattle guard, follow the draw north. The trail at this point overlooks the Front Range, Sugarloaf Mountain (see Hike 37, p. 116), and the rear of Boulder Mountain Parks.

As you meander about the area watch your footing as the trail is rocky. Commonly sighted throughout the Flagstaff Mountain area are coyotes, foxes, mule deer, mountain lions, and raptors. Hike quietly, and be aware that you're more inclined to spot these critters during the early morning and late evening hours. The trails circling the mountain are dotted by wildflowers such as wallflower, larkspur, and penstemon during the spring and summer months.

Continue along the Tenderfoot Trail as it curves around southeast and rambles its way back to Realization Point.

Hiker at lookout point, Tenderfoot Trail, Flagstaff Mountain

Walker Ranch Loop

The surprisingly remote area so close to Boulder makes the Walker Ranch Loop an ideal hike for people seeking solitude, but is a popular mountain biking trail as well.

James Andrew Walker was a Missouri farmer, advised by his doctor to come to Colorado in 1869 to recover from an illness, presumably tuberculosis. After regaining his health and working various jobs in Colorado and Wyoming, he settled in the foothills just west of Boulder. Historical records indicate that Walker and his wife, Phoebe Fidelia Walker, filed a homestead claim on the

original site in 1882, and built it into one of the largest cattle ranches in this region of Colorado. Three generations of the Walker family lived at the ranch. The property was purchased by Boulder County in 1977. The ruins of several old barns and dilapidated structures litter the landscape, adding to the charm of the area.

To begin the hike along this spacious former homestead, park at the South Boulder Creek Trailhead. Locate the trailhead sign and pick up a map of the area describing the various routes.

Columbine Gulch Trail,
Walker Ranch Open Space,
Boulder County Parks and
Open Space

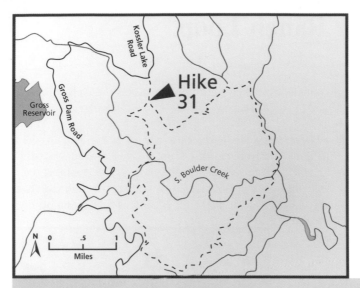

To the trailhead:	From Chautauqua Park, take Baseline Road west (it will merge into Flagstaff Road). Drive 3.3 miles and pass Realization Point. Follow the road another 4.5 miles to the Walker Ranch/South Boulder Creek parking areas.
Distance:	7.6-mile loop
Difficulty:	Easy to moderate
Elevation gain:	940 feet
Dogs:	Yes, under sight and voice command or on leash
Highlights:	Large trailhead kiosk; up-front and close views of the Front Range and Sugarloaf Mountain
Jurisdiction:	City of Boulder Open Space & Mountain Parks

The trail immediately branches right and left. The morning my husband and I hiked it, we opted to take the left side leading east into Crescent Meadows along the Columbine Gulch Trail. It eventually hooks up to the Eldorado Canyon Trail (see Hike 23, p. 81).

Expect a few tight switchbacks as you descend rather steeply directly down to South Boulder Creek, along the canyon floor. The trail is usually alive with athletic mountain bikers. Although trail courtesies require them to yield right-of-way to people on foot, we usually prefer to let the cyclists keep their speed, so we step out of their way.

Forest fire burn area, Columbine Gulch, Walker Ranch Open Space

   The Eldorado Canyon Trail winds along and joins the Crescent Meadows Trail after crossing the creek on a sturdy wooden footbridge. Be sure to bear right; the left-hand trail leads to Eldorado Canyon State Park.

   The Crescent Meadows Trail goes only about 1.75 miles, before you'll take a right onto the South Boulder Creek Trail. You'll cross the creek one more time as the path climbs back up, leading directly to the trailhead, thus completing the loop.

   As this area offers only intermittent shade giving way to wide open skies, cooler temperatures make this a near-perfect hike during the months of September and October.

Meyers Homestead Trail

The Meyers Homestead Trail, on the back side of Flagstaff Mountain neighboring the Walker Ranch property (see Hike 31, p. 101), is a favorite spot of mine to hike and snowshoe. Although close to Boulder, this trail feels like you've stepped back in time to a simpler era, leaving urban stress long forgotten (at least for a while).

The old Walker Ranch is an example of a true Western frontier lifestyle. Around 1900, the major towns and the most productive farms were located along a narrow strip of land we know as the Front Range, a picturesque and pristine place where the mountains meet the plains. Andrew Meyers homesteaded here around 1890, before selling the land to James and Phoebe Walker. Successful cattle breeders, the Walkers built more than a dozen barns, many of which can still be seen from the Meyers Homestead Trail.

Now managed by Boulder County Parks and Open Space, the area is listed on the National Register of Historic Places and is a popular destination for students and teachers during annual Living History Days.

To start the hike, go west from the group picnic area at the parking area for about 0.5 mile, before eventually veering north. When you come upon a fork following a small stream, stay to the right instead of taking the trail that leads to the abandoned barn. The stream will curve away from the trail.

Old barn, Meyers Homestead, Boulder
County Parks and Open Space

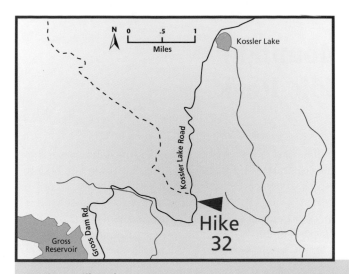

To the trailhead:	From Chautauqua Park, take Baseline Road west (it will merge into Flagstaff Road). Follow Flagstaff Road west up the mountain, driving past Realization Point about 3.3 miles and from there, onward another 4.5 miles to the South Boulder Creek Trailhead parking area.
Distance:	5 miles round-trip
Difficulty:	Easy to moderate
Elevation gain:	600 feet
Dogs:	Yes, on leash
Highlights:	Group picnic area at trailhead; homestead ruins seen from trail; suitable for snowshoeing and cross-country skiing with adequate snowpack
Jurisdiction:	Boulder County Parks and Open Space

Winding and looping through alternating pine and aspen, the route leads to an open meadow, ending at a scenic overlook with views of Boulder Canyon and the Indian Peaks.

In the winter, given adequate snow pack, the Meyers Homestead Trail is a popular place to snowshoe. If you hike during the winter, look for evidence of wildlife showing itself in the form of multiple varieties of tracks in the freshly fallen snow.

Expect significant activity in and around the area during the weekends because of the easily accessible trailhead and the close proximity to Boulder. For solitude, enjoy the trail during weekdays if possible.

Green Mountain and Saddle Rock

Gregory Canyon offers several miles of peaceful and forested terrain. It is here that Green Mountain rises up just behind the Flatirons. The hike to Green Mountain is one of my family's favorites. If you have youngsters 7 or 8 years old, bring them along. The route is popular with grade-schoolers who delight in the thousands of ladybugs that make their home on the summit of Green Mountain during the early spring season.

A gold miner, John Gregory, is said to have built a log road leading to his mines in Black Hawk in this canyon during the 1860s.

Ranger Trail, Green Mountain, City of Boulder Open Space & Mountain Parks

To the trailhead:	From Chautauqua Park, take Baseline Road west; it will merge into Flagstaff Road at the Gregory Canyon Trailhead. Park along the road. Parking fees are charged for vehicles not registered in Boulder County.
Distance:	5 miles round-trip
Difficulty:	Moderately strenuous
Elevation gain:	2,344 feet
Dogs:	Yes, on leash or under voice and sight command
Highlights:	Always popular trail for locals; public facilities at trailhead
Jurisdiction:	City of Boulder Open Space & Mountain Parks

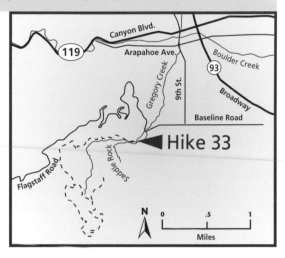

To begin the hike up to Green Mountain, start at the Gregory Canyon Trailhead. Walk west, then immediately veer left, crossing Gregory Creek.

This part of the hike is quite pleasant, surrounded by a fragrant and lush forest of indigenous pine trees and shrubs. Because of the popularity of the trail and proximity to Boulder, the route won't offer much solitude, but it does provide a formidable workout, gaining 2,344 vertical feet in less than 3 miles.

You'll soon turn left (south) to join the Amphitheater Trail. You will ultimately pass a junction leading to Saddle Rock and cross a small ridge with spectacular views. The trail will merge first with Saddle Rock Trail then with the E.M. Greenman Trail at 1.4 miles into the hike.

From here, bear left (south) and continue up Greenman Trail, crossing a small stream called Greenman Springs. Expect some frequent, rocky switchbacks and increasing steepness.

Finally at the summit of Green Mountain, you are welcomed with plenty of sit-down-size sandstone rocks and an impressive cairn-topped viewfinder identifying more than a dozen peaks from north to south. Expect excellent views. You can see the skyline of Denver, all of Boulder, the plains to the east, and the peaks of Rocky Mountain National Park to the north.

After admiring the scenery, you can either come back the way you came or take the right-hand fork on the west ridge of Green Mountain to access Ranger Trail north. Bear right (east) at the fork onto the Greenman Trail, then veer left onto Saddle Rock trail and back to the trailhead.

For another hike option from the same trailhead, you can access Saddle Rock. The 1,250-feet elevation gain rewards you with an exhibition of spectacular rock outcrops dating back thousands of years.

Follow the Gregory Canyon Trail and rather soon, take the left fork, crossing Gregory Creek. The trail leads uphill through a pleasantly dense forest eventually joining the Amphitheater Trail. Be prepared: In some areas the well-maintained route leads you up a steep ascent.

Coming upon another fork, take the trail to your right (west). At this point, expect to see expansive views of Boulder to the east and an unobstructed view of one of Boulder's popular Flatirons.

You will next reach a ridge on the short trail; immediately to the north is Saddle Rock and to the west you can see the Indian Peaks. Some folks opt to do an uncomplicated rock scramble to the actual Saddle Rock. I generally just admire it from the trail.

Another, less strenuous option, if you're not feeling up to a 2,344-foot ascent, is to drive further west up Flagstaff Road 3.3 miles to a three-way intersection and park across from Realization Point. Just walk south, down along an old service road into the forest, and pick up Ranger Trail heading south. Hiking here to Green Mountain's peak gains 1,396 feet in 3.3 miles. Be sure not to take the Long Canyon Trail to the right of Green Mountain's stone lodge, as it will exit back onto Flagstaff Road in 1.1 miles, just south of the Cathedral Park picnic area. Go left past the lodge to Ranger Trail instead. This trail will branch twice more: Just veer right at the first fork, then go left (east) when it hooks up to Green Mountain's west ridge.

Gregory Canyon to Flagstaff Mountain

I smile as I recall my mother's furrowed brows and white knuckles clutching her purse as we drove up the curving and precipitous Flagstaff Road on her first trip to Boulder. Many people reach Flagstaff Mountain by way of its winding, scenic road. In hindsight, I should have offered my mother the opportunity to hike to the summit instead. She was always spry and adventurous, and a hike along the secluded 1.5-mile Flagstaff Trail is an equally good way to enjoy the incredible views.

A hike along the moderately steep trail will not only invigorate you, it will yield a sense of satisfaction perhaps unknown to visitors who've reached the summit via automobile. An added incentive is that the trail is still relatively unknown and little-traveled compared to other trails in and around Boulder. A dentist friend of mine runs and hikes this trail regularly each Wednesday because it is fairly quiet and offers a good, aerobic workout.

Locate the Flagstaff Trailhead on the west side of Gregory Creek after parking with discretion along the road leading into Gregory Canyon. The rocky footpath goes north past the trailhead sign and begins its steep ascent right away. The remote route twists through forests and accesses some incredible views of the City of Boulder.

The only downside to this trail, and maybe why it's not heavily traveled, is that you must cross Flagstaff Road numerous times before reaching the summit. For the most part, I've found that drivers yield to pedestrians at the well-marked crosswalks.

Count your road crossings. Just before Flagstaff Road abuts the trail for the fourth time, take a sharp right and don't cross the road. If you did, you would enter the Crown Rock Trail, with access to the Upper Crown Rock bouldering area.

Passing Flagstaff Road for the fifth time, there are a couple of wonderful flat rocks

Rocky Mountain beeplant, Gregory Canyon Trail, City of Boulder Open Space & Mountain Parks

Foothills

To the trailhead:	From Chautauqua Park, take Baseline Road west to where it merges into Flagstaff Road at the Gregory Canyon Trailhead. Park along the street where permitted. Parking fees are charged for vehicles not registered in Boulder County.
Distance:	3 miles round-trip
Difficulty:	Moderate
Elevation gain:	1,120 feet
Dogs:	Yes, on leash or under voice and sight command
Highlights:	Little-traveled trail; Flagstaff Nature Center at summit; potential for deer sightings
Jurisdiction:	City of Boulder Open Space & Mountain Parks

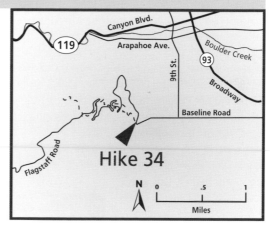

Opposite: Trail near Flagstaff Mountain summit

to rest on, offering an unobstructed view of the plains to the east. On a clear day, the skyline of Denver stands quietly to the south and east. Looking down from that particular spot, you can see a red rock outcropping some locals dub "the Alamo."

Follow the vertical trail all the way to the summit, expecting few switchbacks along the way. The forest at the summit welcomes visitors to explore and rest in its shade. The views of Boulder and the red roofs of the University of Colorado to the east are exceptional. At the top, be sure to locate the Nature Center, seasonally staffed by volunteers.

And you may be pleasantly surprised: Flagstaff's 6,872-foot summit is all the more satisfying having reached it on foot.

Betasso Preserve and Bummers Rock

A trip up Boulder Canyon and a short drive up Sugarloaf Road leads to Betasso Preserve.

The area was originally homesteaded by the Blanchard family in 1912, then later by the Betasso family around 1915. Homestead ruins and antiquated farming equipment can still be seen scattered about the landscape.

The rugged and rustic surroundings are spacious, scenic, and serene. Betasso Preserve is a forested region of fragrant Douglas fir and ponderosa pine. You might choose to either start or end your hike with a snack or lunch as numerous picnic tables and memorial benches embellish the 773-acre backcountry area.

The 3-mile Canyon Loop Trail hike starts at about 6,480 feet and ends there with a net gain and loss of only about 500 feet. This is a multi-use trail for horses, hikers, and cyclists. The several times I've hiked the Canyon Loop Trail, I did not see any horses; plenty of cyclists, however.

Rather than starting your hike from the trailhead downward on the right side of the loop, veer left and hike west. Walking in this direction enables you to watch out for oncoming mountain bikers. But stay alert: Boulder County Parks and Open Space periodically changes the directional signs on this trail for mountain bikers.

Old farm implements along Canyon Loop Trail, Betasso Preserve

After a short climb north and west, you will begin a winding descent through a densely forested area, amid strewn rock on a packed clay path. Follow the trail throughout the quiet, hilly meadows as it bends and loops along the grassy terrain ending back at the trailhead picnic area.

A nice extension of the hike is nearby Bummers Rock Trail. No cyclists

To the trailhead:	From 28th St. (US 36), take Canyon Blvd. (CO 119) west for 6 miles. Turn right (north) onto Sugarloaf Road, then drive for 0.9 mile. Turn right again (east) at Betasso Road, and you will soon come to a fork. The left fork goes to Betasso Preserve and the picnic areas and the right fork to the Bummers Rock Trailhead.
Distance:	3-mile loop
Difficulty:	Easy to moderate
Elevation gain:	500 feet gain and loss
Dogs:	Yes, on leash
Highlights:	Picnic tables; shelter and public facilities at trailhead; at the time of this printing, cyclists are prohibited on the Canyon Loop Trail on Wednesdays and Saturdays (call 303-441-4559 for current policies)
Jurisdiction:	Boulder County Parks and Open Space

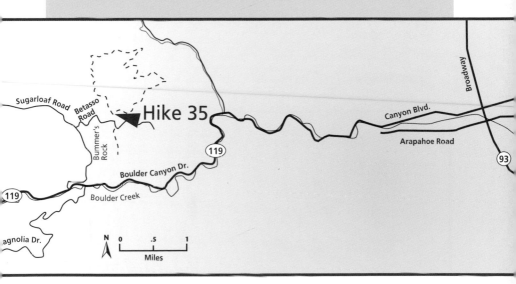

are permitted on this trail at any time. The parking area for Bummers Rock (elevation 6,670 feet) can be accessed by following the fork near the entrance at right and traveling a bit further south of the Betasso Preserve Trailhead parking area. This route offers an easy 0.6 mile round-trip hike to a scenic overlook of the surrounding canyon.

Mount Sanitas

A mere 6,863-foot at its summit, Mount Sanitas is sometimes snubbed by true peak-baggers. That's okay, because the 3.1-mile loop gaining 1,343 vertical feet offers hikers a formidable workout without the tedious drive from Boulder to a fourteener trailhead.

To the trailhead:	From north Broadway (CO93), go west on Mapleton Ave. past Fourth St. Look for the large Centennial Trailhead parking area on your left abutting Sunshine Canyon.
Distance:	3.1-mile loop
Difficulty:	Moderate
Elevation gain:	1,343 feet
Dogs:	Yes, on leash
Highlights:	Picnic pavilion; rugged trail conveniently located
Jurisdiction:	City of Boulder Open Space & Mountain Parks

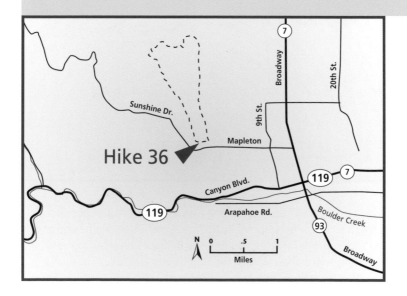

Mount Sanitas is named for the Boulder Sanitarium, built in 1895, that is now the Mapleton Medical Center. Sandstone quarried near Mount Sanitas was used to build a number of University of Colorado buildings.

Start your hike at the parking area just past the pavilion housing picnic tables. Cross over a small bridge and head north to the main trail. You'll be at a trail junction: The Mount Sanitas Trail is on the left, the Sanitas Valley Trail to the right. Veer left to hike up the south ridge.

Log stairs and large stepping stones on the well-maintained Mount Sanitas Trail lead you up the vertical ascent graced by several false summits.

The ridge plateaus briefly in spots so you can catch your breath. Don't be embarrassed if it's necessary to stop occasionally; although much shorter, Mount Sanitas is steeper than some Colorado fourteener trails. It's a straight shot the entire way to the top.

Dakota Valley Trail, Dakota Ridge, City of Boulder Open Space & Mountain Parks

At the rocky summit, you can perch yourself on one of the large boulders to relax and enjoy panoramic views in all directions.

As you look down and east from the Mount Sanitas Trail, and from the summit as well, you can see the mile-long Dakota Ridge Trail at the edge of the forest parallel to the Sanitas Valley Trail. The Dakota Ridge Trail starts 0.3 mile east of the Sanitas Valley Trail off of Mapleton Avenue and intersects the Sanitas Valley Trail at its northern end.

From the Mount Sanitas summit, return the way you came or hike slightly east and south to access the Sanitas Valley Trail back to the parking area.

Foothills

Sugarloaf Mountain

Webster's *New World Dictionary* defines "escape" as the act of "getting free," and that's truly what outdoor enthusiasts experience when hiking Sugarloaf Mountain. The plains seemingly flow endlessly to the east viewed from the summit of 8,917-foot Sugarloaf Mountain, and the jagged summits of the Indian Peaks stand tall to the west. It's an arresting vista. Views from its summit also encompass the Mummy Range, Longs Peak, and Mount Evans.

This is a pretty straightforward hike, gaining not quite 500 feet in about 1 mile, along an old, cobbled, rocky roadbed that serves as the trail. The wide-open, windswept summit drops away precipitously along Sugarloaf's conical, symmetrical flanks.

Gnarly tree, Sugarloaf Mountain summit, Boulder County Parks and Open Space

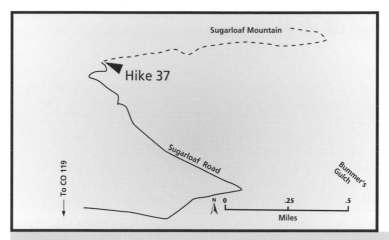

To the trailhead:	From 28th St. (US 36), take Canyon Blvd. (CO 119) west for 5.3 miles to Sugarloaf Road. Turn right (north) and drive 4.9 miles up to Sugarloaf Mountain Road. Turn right (east) for 0.8 mile to the parking area.
Distance:	2 miles round-trip
Difficulty:	Easy
Elevation gain:	477 feet
Dogs:	Yes, on leash
Highlights:	Easy hike yields spectacular views; nice outing with kids
Jurisdiction:	Boulder County Parks and Open Space

As you make your way north along the trail, traversing three switchbacks, don't worry about any forks you encounter, as they will reemerge again. Although it's a fairly easy hike with little elevation gain, Sugarloaf Mountain gets a significant amount of foot traffic throughout the year because of its easily accessible trailhead and close proximity to Boulder.

At the trailhead parking lot, a connection to the Switzerland Trail heads west toward Glacier Lake.

Foothills

Boulder Falls

Although it isn't really a hike, Boulder Falls is the place some of us go when we are out of tune and need to be brought back to harmony. Just a short and scenic drive nestled in a bend along Boulder Canyon, it is a local favorite, familiar and comforting to many. The tucked-away falls are a dependable medicine, a soothing remedy, and a not-so-hidden gem.

"The settlers found Boulder Canyon so difficult to access that a man could not make his way up it by foot. ...It was a disputed question whether or not a wagon road could ever be constructed through it," according to Boulder historian Amos Bixby.

A rough and bumpy toll road was built up Boulder Canyon leading to Magnolia Road in 1865, although it was not extended to Nederland (then called Middle Boulder) until 1871. Years ago Charles G. Buckingham gave five acres of old mining claims, including the dramatic Boulder Falls area, to the City of Boulder. Closed briefly during April 2003 for restoration and repair work, the refurbished short trail is now safer for visitors. Several large, unstable boulders above the trail were removed. City of Boulder staff working with an AmeriCorps crew performed the cleanup and maintenance work on the trail.

For obvious safety reasons, the area beyond the viewpoint remains closed. Be advised to follow the safety precautions posted in and around the falls. The rocks and water past this point are deceptively dangerous, and numerous unfortunate accidents have befallen visitors scrambling around the falls.

Rocky crags, jagged outcrops, and the powerful falls, not to mention the occasional rock climber or two you're bound to spot rappelling high on the cliffs above, are some of the splendid features you'll see when visiting Boulder Falls.

Opposite: Boulder Falls, North Boulder Creek, City of Boulder Open Space & Mountain Parks

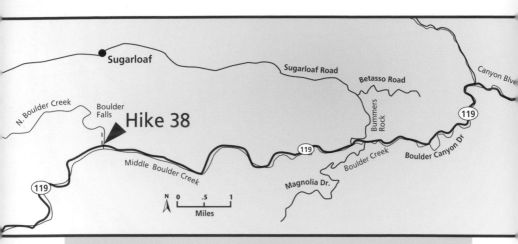

To the trailhead:	The pull-off for the falls is located 11 miles west of Boulder on Canyon Blvd. (CO 119), between Boulder and Nederland. Parking is on the south side; the falls are located to the north.
Distance:	Less than a 0.25 mile
Difficulty:	Easy
Elevation gain:	Negligible
Dogs:	Yes, on leash
Highlights:	The falls tumble down boldly; bring a camera to photograph the hollow rock near the large kiosk
Jurisdiction:	City of Boulder Open Space & Mountain Parks

Picture Rock is a large gray boulder located just next to the road at Boulder Falls, across from the parking area. The rock has been naturally eroded to produce the circular opening for which it was named. It was hauled up from Boulder Creek when the new roadway was built in the 1940s. I have an adorable picture of my son smiling brightly when he was just a toddler, kneeling within and peeking out from the hole in that rock.

While small in terms of acreage, the Boulder Falls area is a delightful getaway offering one of the most remarkable creations of nature so close to the city.

Bald Mountain

First opened in 1973 as a public park, the 108-acre Bald Mountain Scenic Area takes its name from the fact that few trees thrive at its windswept 7,160-foot summit. As if that's not enough, in the mid-1970s the mountain pine beetle epidemic spread to the area, infecting hundreds of trees. Diseased trees were cut and fumigated in the western side of the park. The beetle problem came under control by 1980 because of the decrease in the insect population and forest management actions.

Despite the lack of trees, Bald Mountain's spacious and picturesque summit beckons families with small children, retired couples, folks from the flat lands, and others looking for a tranquil getaway and easy hike.

A sizeable park bench is strategically located at the summit of Bald Mountain, allowing for an unobstructed view of Green and Bear Mountains, and South Boulder Peak to the east. The Continental Divide stands tall and serene to the west. The Pines-to-Peak Trail accessed from the summit offers visitors a short and scenic loop through scattered ponderosa pine forests and seasonal wildflower meadows.

View of Green Mountain from Bald Mountain summit, Pines to Peak Trail, Boulder County Parks and Open Space

An old-fashioned livestock corral and loading chute stand near the park's entrance, a remnant of the old Jones' 1886 homestead, no longer a farm. Deer have replaced cows along its high slopes and spacious meadow.

This is an ideal off-season hike throughout the year, with its easy 240-foot elevation gain. The Bald Mountain Scenic Area is also a good place to take family and friends from out of town who are not acclimated to Colorado's higher elevations.

Foothills

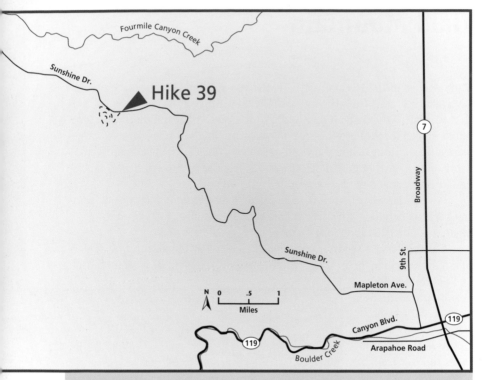

To the trailhead:	From Broadway (CO7), go west on Mapleton Ave. until it turns into Sunshine Canyon Drive (CR 52). The trailhead is on the left (south) side of the road.
Distance:	1.5-mile loop
Difficulty:	Easy
Elevation gain:	240 feet
Dogs:	Yes, on leash
Highlights:	The Bald Mountain Scenic Area is a public park open from sunrise to sunset and camping is prohibited; plenty of picnic tables, ample parking, and a toilet facility are available
Jurisdiction:	Boulder County Parks and Open Space

Anne U. White Trail

Spring runoff, Four Mile Creek,
Anne U. White Trail, Boulder
County Parks and Open Space

Access to the short and easy Anne Underwood White Trail in Fourmile Canyon Creek Park is easy to miss because of its tucked-away location. The trail is named for the Boulder civic activist who advocated for open space and other worthy causes. Parking is quite limited, so enjoy this trail during weekday mornings or early evenings, if possible.

The route offers a sustained but gradual 540-foot elevation gain. Unlike routes elsewhere, the Anne U. White Trail probably is not suitable for snow shoeing during the winter because of numerous stream crossings.

Once at the trail, zigzagging along Fourmile Canyon Creek, you can expect to cross the stream many times until it ends at private property denoted with signage and barbed-wire fences.

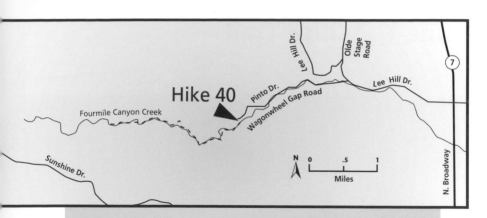

To the trailhead:	Take N. Broadway (CO 7) north to Lee Hill Road. Turn left (west) and drive about 1 mile to Wagonwheel Gap Road. Turn left (south) and drive 1 mile to Pinto Dr., a packed gravel road. Turn left (east) and park at the designated trailhead where the road dead-ends. Parking is limited to three vehicles.
Distance:	1.5 miles one-way
Difficulty:	Easy
Elevation gain:	560 feet
Dogs:	Yes, on leash
Highlights:	Quiet forested trail rambling alongside a creek
Jurisdiction:	Boulder County Parks and Open Space

While hiking here, you needn't worry about wearing waterproof boots as the stream crossings have plenty of large stepping stones in place. The tiny trickle and hum of the water in spots is alluring and adds to the feeling of serenity and quiet awe along the route that permeates Fourmile Canyon Creek Park.

About halfway along the footpath, expect to come upon a small, pink flagstone bench overlooking the creek.

Once you've hiked some 30 or 45 minutes—depending on your speed, of course—you will come to the end of the short 1.5-mile trail, just under some rock outcroppings. Turn around and return the way you came.

Opposite: Small waterfall, Four Mile Creek, Anne U. White Trail, Boulder County Parks and Open Space

Heil Valley Ranch

The newly created trails meandering through Heil Valley Ranch are canopied with lush, fragrant pine trees and dotted with remnants of homestead ruins. The 4,923-acre region is a dedicated wildlife habitat: A herd of elk migrates from the Indian Peaks Wilderness Area (see p. 212) to Heil Valley Ranch each winter.

Boulder County purchased Heil Ranch in 1996, as part of the attractive North Foothills Open Space. Boulder County Youth Corps assisted in forest and trail improvements in part with Colorado Lottery funds.

The Heil family still owns and operates a working farm south of the trailhead, so visitors are advised to be mindful of driving speeds, watching out for strolling livestock along Geer Canyon Drive.

The day my friends and I hiked here, we chose the Wapiti Trail connecting with the Ponderosa Loop, making the expedition a pleasant 7.6 miles. Mountain bikers and pedestrians all along the way were courteous to each other that day, and a pair of unhurried horses with their riders explored the area. The attraction for some visiting here is the no-dog rule: Mountain bikes, runners, equestrians, and hikers only. Dogs are not permitted.

Heading north from the trailhead at an elevation of about 6,000 feet, walk along an old jeep road and veer left onto Wapiti Trail, passing a large prairie dog colony. You'll quickly wind into the forest, encountering the steepest part of the hike.

Further north, you'll cross another service road and soon come upon some old sandstone ruins of a building at 6,621 feet.

Lichen-covered boulders, Lichen Trail, Heil Ranch Open Space

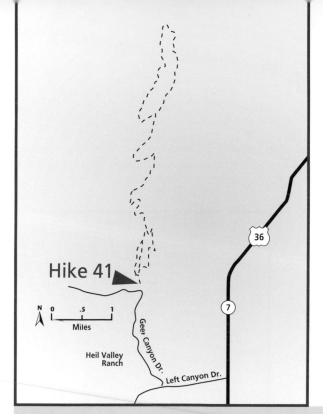

Hike 41

N 0 .5 1
Miles

36

7

Geer Canyon Dr.

Heil Valley
Ranch

Left Canyon Dr.

To the trailhead:	Take Foothills Hwy. (US 36/CO 7) north to Lefthand Canyon Dr. Turn left (west). Take a right (north) at the Heil Valley Ranch sign on Geer Canyon Dr. Drive slowly up the short dirt road to the trailhead parking.
Distance:	7.6 miles round-trip
Difficulty:	Easy to moderate
Elevation gain:	800 feet
Dogs:	No
Highlights:	Prairie dog colony; old sandstone structural ruins; picnic shelters; public facilities
Jurisdiction:	Boulder County Parks and Open Space

Continuing on, the Ponderosa Loop forks left and right. Taking either path offers a relatively flat 2.6-mile roundabout. Stop at the Overlook, surely the most scenic part of this area.

There is also the ideal family-friendly, pedestrian-only, 1-mile Lichen Loop near the trailhead, with picnic shelters and public facilities. This option is well-suited for out-of-town flatlanders, seniors, and families with small children.

Hall Ranch

With a towering mountain backdrop and 3,205 acres of open, rolling meadows, Hall Ranch near Lyons offers equestrians, mountain bikers, and trail hikers all there is to love about Colorado.

This is where the Great Plains meet the southern Rocky Mountains and where millions of years ago, hard tan-colored quartz sandstone was formed. About 20 families lived and worked this area, decades ago. Some farmed, some prospected, and some quarried the sandstone. Several of the buildings at the University of Colorado were built with this attractive and weather-resistant stone.

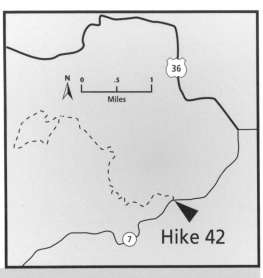

To the trailhead:	From Boulder, take N. Foothills Hwy. (US 36) north from Boulder 11 miles to Lyons. Turn left on CO 66. Where the road forks on CO 7, go left (south) for 1.5 miles to the Hall Ranch Trailhead on the north side of the street. There is ample parking. The area is open from sunrise to sunset.
Distance:	Varies
Difficulty:	Easy to moderate, depending on length
Elevation gain:	1,380 feet gain and loss
Dogs:	No
Highlights:	Picnic tables and public facilities; group shelter accommodating up to 50 people on a first-come, first-serve basis; historic Nelson Ranch homestead
Jurisdiction:	Boulder County Parks and Open Space

View to the southwest, Bitterbrush
Trail, Hall Ranch Open Space

Hall Ranch is now a quiet and peaceful area with wildlife such as jackrabbits, marmots, red and gray foxes, and coyotes. The area was opened to the public in 1996, following a 1993 open space sales tax of 0.25 percent approved by Boulder County voters.

Hall Ranch, with more than 12 miles of multi-use trails, is home to the Bitterbrush Trail (3.7 miles) and Nelson Loop (2.2 miles), while the Nighthawk Trail (4.7 miles) and Button Rock Trail (2 miles) complete the trail system. Because of equestrians and mountain bike enthusiasts, and in an effort to maintain the area as a haven for wildlife, dogs are not permitted on the trails.

Beware of extreme heat during July and August; be sure to bring ample water and sunscreen. Also watch out for rattlesnakes between the months of March and October.

To start the hike, begin walking south and east from the trailhead on the Bitterbrush Trail. Do not veer off onto the Nighthawk Trail. Expect gradual elevation gain throughout the hike.

The pleasant, winding trail gently rises and dips, eventually connecting with the Nelson Loop Trail at about 4 miles into the hike. There are several big rocks suitable for resting on.

Take the left-hand fork south. Soon you'll take the right fork of the trail leading west to the historic Nelson Ranch homestead.

As you come around on the Nelson Loop Trail and catch up with the Bitterbrush Trail to your right, you'll spot a large prairie dog town spilling down into the meadow. Because of critical wildlife habitat protection, the trail skirts around it and adds what seems like miles to your hike. But it's captivating to observe the prairie dog colony at work and play.

Rabbit Mountain

With acres and acres of open space surrounding it, Rabbit Mountain is often overlooked by seasoned hikers. Maybe that's because it is a short hike, only about 2 miles out and back, gaining just 500 feet. But the vistas atop the small mountain rival any from elsewhere in Boulder.

From its summit you can see all of Boulder Valley to the south and the St. Vrain River Valley to the east. The view from the top also includes Longs Peak and Mount Meeker in Rocky Mountain National Park and the peach and salmon colors of the rock formations that make up Little Thompson Canyon. The sign at the top indicates Little Thompson Overlook, named for the Little Thompson River to the north. On a clear day from some locations along the trail you can even see Pikes Peak way to the south.

Boulder County Parks and Open Space obtained the area in 1984 from the granddaughter of National Park Service Ranger Jack Moomaw. He was one of the first National Park Service Rangers east of the Continental Divide.

To begin the trek, locate the map at the trailhead kiosk. Arrive early, as the parking lot fills up fast on weekends. The Little Thompson Overlook Trail winds up the rocky swell of the mountain near a wide, gravel service road.

At the signpost, turn left (west) and climb up to the overlook. Alternatively, a spur along the 3-mile Eagle Wind Trail goes right (east) along the mesa from the main trail, offering excellent views as well.

Rabbit Mountain was once called Rattlesnake Mountain for a reason. Look out for rattlers and bull snakes along the trail and in the brush. Wear hiking boots that cover your ankles. And, because the area is well-known as a cycling destination, be mindful of eager bikers coming and going throughout the area.

Eagle Wind Trail, Rabbit Mountain Open Space

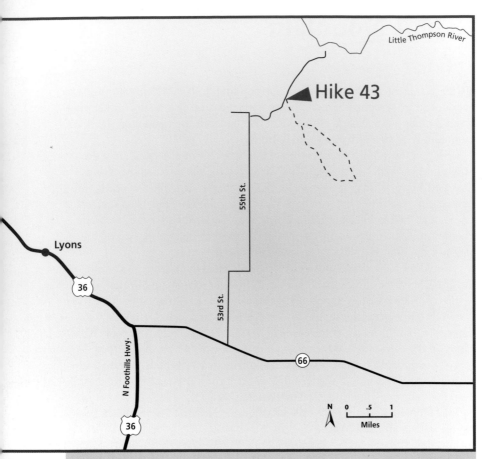

Little Thompson River

Hike 43

55th St.

Lyons

36

53rd St.

N Foothills Hwy.

66

36

N   0   .5   1
Miles

To the trailhead:	From Boulder, take N. Foothills Hwy. (US 36) north 11 miles to Lyons. Turn right on CO 66. Drive 1 mile to 53rd St. Turn left and go 2 miles to the trailhead on your right.
Distance:	2 miles round-trip
Difficulty:	Easy to moderate
Elevation gain:	About 400 feet
Dogs:	Yes, on leash
Highlights:	Public facilities; picnic shelter near the trailhead
Jurisdiction:	Boulder County Parks and Open Space

Big Elk Meadows

North Saint Vrain Creek, Coulson Gulch
Trail, near Ralph Price Reservoir

Touted as one of the wildest places in and around Boulder County, Big Elk Meadows is truly untamed and unforgettable. And a trip along the Coulson Gulch Trail in Big Elk Meadows satisfies the urge to get away and really feel as if you've escaped civilization. While walking in this seemingly remote area, be

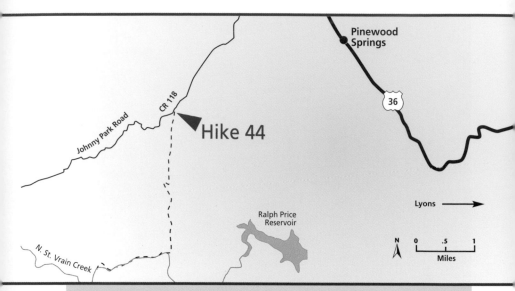

To the trailhead:	From Boulder, take US 36 north through Lyons. Drive 9.6 miles past town to the Big Elk Meadows turnoff (CR 118). Turn left (west) and follow the winding road for about 5 miles to a Y-junction. Take the left fork up a bumpy, gravel road 0.5 mile to the Coulson Gulch Trailhead.
Distance:	5.6 miles round-trip
Difficulty:	Easy
Elevation gain:	900 feet
Dogs:	Yes, on leash
Highlights:	Rustic ruins of a log cabin nestled in the forest; ideal picnic spots near bridge
Jurisdiction:	Boulder Ranger District, Arapaho and Roosevelt National Forests

Near Higgins Park, along Coulson Gulch Trail, Big Elk Meadows

mindful to touch the land lightly and keep Big Elk Meadows wild. Additionally, if you're hiking during Colorado's fall hunting season—late August to early January—be sure to wear bright-colored clothing.

To begin the hike, from the large parking area take the narrow trail just past the three tall wooden poles. This packed-dirt and sandy footpath will drop steadily south along Coulson Gulch, eventually spilling into Higgins Park.

The trail is not steep and has few switchbacks, although expect to descend several hundred feet. Just before you reach Higgins Park, to the right of the trail, keep a lookout for the enchanting ruins of a log cabin. Inside is a rusted bed frame leaning against the weathered structure, and just outside of the cabin is an antiquated stove.

The meadow spreads open, trees growing from grasses and shrubs. From Higgins Park, the trail joins the old Button Rock jeep road, which is no longer open to vehicles. Immediately to the left of the trail, South Sheep Mountain stands alone.

At the trail junction, turn right (west). After about 20 minutes or so, expect to cross a large wooden footbridge over North St. Vrain Creek. The trail hugs along the creek and eventually another bridge crosses it.

About 2.8 miles into the area, having gained 900 feet in elevation, you have found a good spot to eat a leisurely lunch. Then turn around and return the way you came.

Button Rock Preserve

Looking for a short hike to an ideal picnic spot? Situated in a quiet river valley about 7 miles west of Lyons, Button Rock Preserve offers an interesting oasis for people and wildlife alike. The preserve is the City of Longmont's watershed area and home to the Ralph Price Reservoir (named for a former Longmont mayor) and the smaller Longmont Reservoir.

Because of the negligible elevation gain on Longmont Dam Road and available restrooms, a part of the preserve is ideal for families, strollers, classroom field trips, and wheelchair users.

Ponderosa pine framing Mount Meeker and Longs Peak, Sleepy Lion Trail, Button Rock Preserve

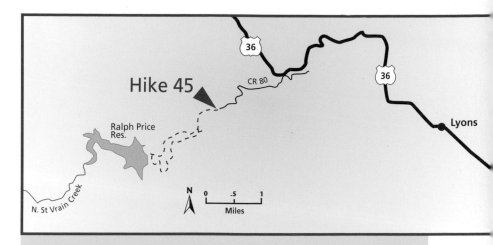

To the trailhead:	From Boulder, take US 36 north through Lyons. Four miles out of town, turn left (west) at CR 80. Continue for 2.8 miles to the entrance of Button Rock Preserve.
Distance:	4 miles round-trip
Difficulty:	Easy
Elevation gain:	300-feet
Dogs:	Yes, on leash
Highlights:	Public facilities; wheelchair accessible in areas; special fishing permit required to fish from the shoreline, May through October, limited number issued annually by Longmont City Clerk's office
Jurisdiction:	City of Longmont, Button Rock Ranger Station

To begin the hike, you'll walk west along the road (closed to traffic except for authorized vehicles) for about 1 mile, passing Longmont Reservoir on the right. The soothing roar and hum of North St. Vrain Creek fills the air. At about this spot you'll come to a sign on your left indicating Sleepy Lion Trail. Presumably, this particular trail was affectionately named decades ago for a mountain lion seen napping there.

Sleepy Lion Trail offers a 500-foot elevation gain along the 2-mile route through a ponderosa pine and Douglas fir forest and an open meadow. Just before this trail drops to Ralph Price Reservoir, the Button Rock Trail links to Nighthawk Trail and Hall Ranch (see Hike 42, p. 128). The reservoir is stocked

Sleepy Lion Trail, Button Rock Preserve

with brown and rainbow trout
and with splake (a brook and
lake trout hybrid), but a special fishing permit is required.

If you want to extend your hike for only 1 more mile, rather than taking Sleepy Lion Trail continue on the shorter, more direct route to the reservoir straight ahead on Longmont Dam Road, turning right after reaching the dam and climbing briefly, zigzagging for 300 feet. This is the steepest part of the trail.

A 3-mile trail extends along the right side of the reservoir, heading to an inlet on the northwest end. But really anywhere throughout the preserve makes for a pleasant place to picnic and complete your hike.

Button Rock Preserve offers an escape from the usual crowding at other nearby reservoirs.

Lion Gulch to Homestead Meadows

Much of Colorado is so rugged that our state was settled years later than surrounding areas—the harsh winters and steep mountains dissuaded potential homesteaders. But fortunately not all of them. Roosevelt National Forest's Homestead Meadows is a scenic testament to this pioneering spirit. The Lion Gulch Trail between Estes Park and Pinewood Springs leads to the large, homesteaded meadow.

Eight hardy homesteaders settled there from 1889 to 1923. The families include: Brown, Irvin, Griffith, Hill, Engert, Laycock, and Boren. A lone British woman, Sarah Walker, also built her cabin at Homestead Meadows after outliving her husband and children. The Big Elk Fire destroyed the Engert historical structure in July 2002.

The area is now designated a National Historic District. It's rich in history, abutting Rocky Mountain National Park to the north. Numerous interpretive signs share the settlers' stories.

The Lion Gulch Trail is a moderate hike ascending through the Roosevelt National Forest eventually leading to Homestead Meadows, where the historical homesteads still remain. It is 2.7 miles to the first site; the length of the hike increases to 6.5 miles if all the homesteads are visited.

The trail is open to hikers, mountain bikers, and horseback riders. It is a dog-friendly trail, too. The Lion Gulch trail also accesses Pierson Park.

Begin at about 7,320-feet elevation, parking at the large trailhead on the south side of US 36. A poignant flag memorial is placed near the informational kiosk in memory of the two men flying Tanker 123, which crashed in the Big Elk Fire.

The trail starts by dropping down via a few switchbacks to a creek. After crossing the first bridge, veer right, proceeding to climb. You can opt to take the right-hand horse turnoff along the path for a brief time or continue on the designated hiking trail.

The dusty and rocky footpath continues upward in the shade of towering pines. Expect only one steep portion about a third of the way into the forested canyon. You'll cross the creek numerous times on log bridges. You may see numerous equestrians on the trail, as it is popular with horse traffic.

As you reach the end of the trail, it opens up into the long and wide Homestead Meadows where you can begin your gentle voyage back through time amongst the log cabin ruins. You reach Homestead Meadows in about 3 miles and can crisscross to the worn and weathered cabins, adding additional miles to your hike as you explore the variety of homesteads.

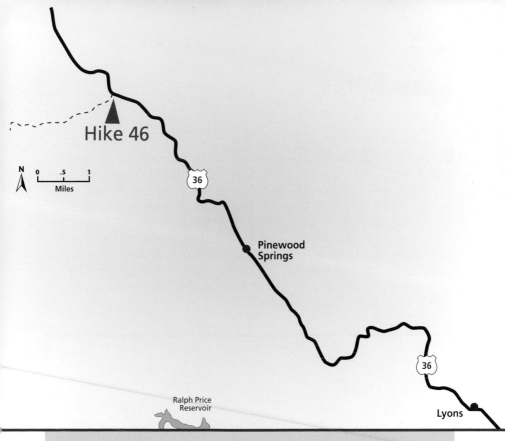

Hike 46

N

0   .5   1
Miles

36

Pinewood
Springs

36

Ralph Price
Reservoir

Lyons

To the trailhead:	The Lion Gulch/Homestead Meadows Trailhead is located 12 miles northwest of Lyons. From Boulder, take US 36 north through Lyons. Continue on the highway for about 7 miles past Pinewood Springs. The trailhead is on the south side of US 36.
Distance:	6 miles round trip
Difficulty:	Easy to moderate
Elevation gain:	1,300 feet
Dogs:	Yes
Highlights:	National Historic District containing original homesteaders' cabins in a quiet meadow; numerous interpretive signs; equestrians welcome
Jurisdiction:	Canyon Lakes Ranger District, Arapaho and Roosevelt National Forests

Opposite: Cabin at Homestead Meadow, Lion Gulch Trail, Roosevelt National Forest

Lake Estes

Between the flatlands to the east and the majestic mountains to the west, the small resort village of Estes Park is blessed with outstanding beauty and diversity. Nearby Lake Estes provides residents and visitors memorable experiences boating, fishing, hiking, or simply sunning themselves on the small beach.

For a quick study in Rocky Mountain recreation, you could hardly find better instruction than here. Lake Estes is snuggled up against many of the best hiking trails twisting through Rocky Mountain National Park (see page 148). But the lake also offers a fine trail of its own, circling the water for 3.8 miles. The trail hugging Lake Estes, at an elevation of 7,475 feet, was a phased project begun in 1994 and completed in 2000.

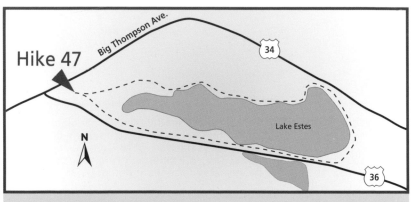

To the trailhead:	Take US 36 north from Boulder to Estes Park. Turn right on Big Thompson Ave. (a left turn takes you on Elkhorn Ave.). Access the trail at the Visitor Center parking lot.
Distance:	3.8-mile loop around the lake
Difficulty:	Easy
Elevation gain:	Negligible
Dogs:	Yes, on leash
Highlights:	Fishing permitted; state license required; wheelchair accessible; Visitor Center; bird sanctuary
Jurisdiction:	Estes Valley Recreation & Park District, 970-586-8191

Bighorn Mountain, from
Lake Estes Trail, Estes Park

Foothills

In and around Lake Estes, especially during the fall season, is one of the best places to observe elk. Along the paved path, the trail itself is wheelchair accessible. A popular starting place (although there are several circling the lake) is at the Visitor Center off Big Thompson Ave. As you start from this location, you will pass a bird sanctuary positioned in a small, dedicated wetland section. Large, buff-brown colored elk have been seen here resting in the shade by the creek.

The large body of water is framed with a flat, easy trail, revealing sights of Twin Sisters Peaks to the south, while the Continental Divide towers over the western horizon. As you make your way around the lake, you'll come to the lake marina store. The shop sells fishing licenses, fishing supplies, snacks, and sun products.

The trail drops between 70 and 100 feet into Wapiti Meadows at the southern end of the reservoir. Even on sunny and warm days, a sweater or light jacket may be necessary as the wind whips over and through the canyons of the neighboring peaks.

An extension of the existing trail is in the works, connecting the Lake Estes path to CO 7 and Fish Creek Trails, ultimately creating a figure eight.

If you've come to Lake Estes seeking stillness and peace, you may be disappointed. However, if you're visiting the lake to enjoy being outdoors and take pleasure in people-watching, then this is the place for you.

Caribou Ranch Open Space

Some say Boulder County's newest open space property, Caribou Ranch, is its crown jewel. Made up of 2,180 acres of designated open space, with charming homestead and mining ruins, perhaps part of the allure is that it is the county's only high-mountain park.

The trail is about 4.5 miles out and back, offering a pleasant, forested loop in the montane ecological zone. Because of the lack of elevation gain, and the fact that more than half of the route is on a road, Caribou Ranch may not appeal to hikers who value more rugged terrain.

A herd of some 175 elk makes use of the property as a transitional range in spring and fall. In fact, permanent spring closures are in effect April 1 through June 30 to protect spring migratory birds, overwinter elk survival, and elk calving and rearing activities. During a study of elk behavior and movements in September 2005, visitors will only be allowed to travel to an elk overlook, about 0.75 mile from the trailhead. Visitor compliance during these closures is crucial.

To start the hike, walk northwest from the parking lot on the DeLonde Trail into the forest. As you ramble along the newly built trail, it will fork in 1.2 miles. If you stay straight, you'll

Trail to DeLonde Homestead, Caribou Ranch Open Space

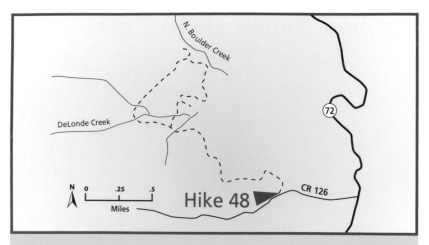

N   0   .25   .5
Miles

CR 126

Hike 48 ▼

To the trailhead:	Take Canyon Blvd. (CO 119) west from Boulder to Nederland. Turn right (north) on the Peak-to-Peak Highway (CO 72). Go 1.9 miles to CR 126. Turn left (west) and drive 0.9 mile to the parking area on your right. (The Caribou Ranch Open Space area is different than the historical Caribou town site, located just west of Nederland on CR 138.)
Distance:	About 4.5 miles round-trip
Difficulty:	Easy
Elevation gain:	Negligible
Dogs:	No
Highlights:	Mining and homestead ruins; level trail with minimal elevation change; seasonal elk herd viewing; picnic tables; public facilities at large trailhead parking area
Jurisdiction:	Boulder County Parks and Open Space

continue on the road, eventually veering north, accessing the Blue Bird Loop. The elevation gain is negligible and stays steady at about 8,600 feet.

To your right is the DeLonde Homestead, showcasing the ranch's development, with its crib-logged barn. Continuing along the road instead of the side trip to the homestead, you'll soon come upon the old Blue Bird Mine. The mine was served by the Denver, Boulder & Western Railroad and is listed on the National Register of Historic Places as a Historic District. Take the short segue left to the mine where an informational sign describes the area.

As you continue east, you'll be offered the opportunity to step down along the steps to the rocky shore of North Boulder Creek, or walk on, looping around south to make your way back to the DeLonde Homestead site.

Take a stop at this point and leisurely look around at your surroundings. Imagine a place where the living was tough but the ambience was its own reward. Take in the mystique of 1800s farming and mining life in this high mountain valley. The simple main house was built in the 1870s and the barn is currently under reconstruction.

From here, head back to the DeLonde Trail and walk south and east back to the trailhead.

DeLonde Homestead, Caribou Ranch
Open Space

Mountains

The tallest mountains of the Continental Divide cut the state in half with a two-mile-high crest. This rocky impediment has long served as a tribal and intracontinental boundary and as a barrier to exploration and settlement. But not any more.

The Rocky Mountains have evolved from the most rugged and remote frontier into a thriving agricultural, mining, and high-tech hub. Today, our mountains serve as the Front Range backyard playground, enticing adventurers every day in so many ways.

However, an outing to the mountains warrants careful consideration. Mountain hiking is different than walking in city parks. Both experiences yield the immense satisfaction of enjoying the outdoors, but that's about the extent of the similarities.

Rocky Mountain National Park

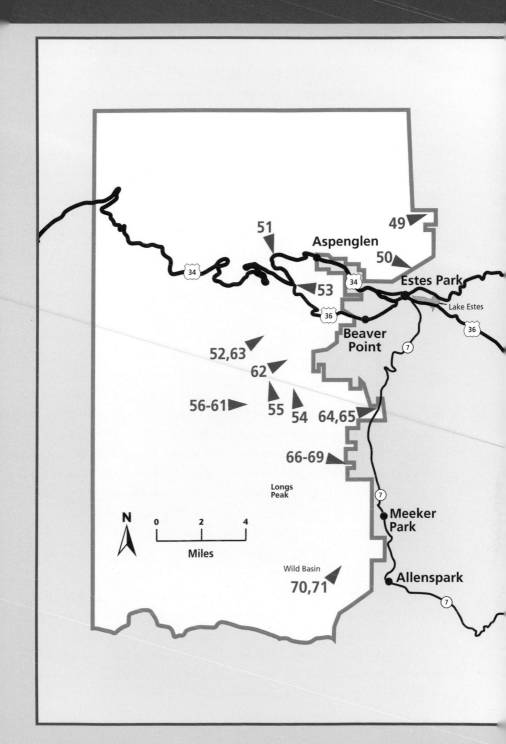

49

51

Aspenglen

50

Estes Park

53

Lake Estes

Beaver
Point

52,63

62

56-61

55

54

64,65

66-69

Longs
Peak

N

0   2   4

Miles

Wild Basin

70,71

Meeker
Park

Allenspark

When hiking in the mountains, it's important to be prepared for unexpected emergencies. For the most part, when walking in and around the city, your car (or shelter) is relatively nearby. But when in the backcountry, you may be miles and miles from cover. For that reason, at the very minimum you must carry survival essentials such as water, snacks, extra layers of clothing, gloves, and a hat. (See p. 19 for a list of suggestions.) For every 984 feet you go up a mountain, the temperature drops by 3.6 degrees. So if you're planning a hike gaining about 3,000 vertical feet, count on your destination being a bit cooler—about 10 degrees—than where you began. Also, weather changes much more rapidly in the high country than in the flatlands.

> "A man does not climb a mountain without bringing some of it away with him and leaving something of himself upon it."
>
> —*Sir Martin Conway*

I'm not a particularly strong hiker, but neither am I weak or casual, and it generally takes me an hour to climb 1,000 to 1,200 vertical feet at a moderate pace. Knowing this, I can plan the time I will reach my destination. For instance, when hiking to Diamond Lake, I can expect to climb the 2 miles and 951 feet in about an hour; the round-trip takes a little over two hours. I usually leave the trailhead about 8 a.m. to be sure to complete the hike before the usual high-country afternoon weather rolls in. No outing is worth the risk of being caught in an electrical storm or blizzard at high elevations and miles from your car.

It's important to note the importance of being alert to wildlife at all times when in the backcountry. You're treading in their territory, not vice versa. Superlatives fail to describe the joy in spotting a bear or group of deer when out hiking. However, do not disturb wildlife and remember to respect the area. Mountain hiking is not without risk. Be prepared to meet the challenges.

Colorado's moderate year-round temperatures combined with the rugged and pristine beauty of mountainous terrain make hiking a near-perfect, soul-soothing sport, particularly at higher elevations.

Rocky Mountain National Park

Rocky Mountain National Park (RMNP) has always been a crossroads of sorts for pioneering explorers long ago and for backcountry travelers and sightseeing visitors today. A conservative estimate indicates that some three million visitors hike, picnic, and drive through the 415-square-mile park each year.

RMNP was created in 1915 after wilderness advocates, led by naturalist Enos Mills and the Colorado Mountain Club, convinced Coloradans that the scenic park would be a beneficial alternative to commercial uses of the land. President Woodrow Wilson declared Rocky Mountain the country's tenth national park. The National Park Service, an agency of the U.S. Department of the Interior that administers our national parks, was formed in 1916.

"I envision national parks as...models of respect for all land and water and all of life," wrote environmentalist Michael Frome, Ph.D. Fortunately for today's outdoor enthusiasts, RMNP also provides a spacious wilderness playground. With hundreds of miles of backcountry trails, located less than 40 miles from downtown Boulder, it is a favorite among local hikers and backpackers.

The park is made up of more than 60 mountains that soar above 12,000 feet. In fact, one-third of the park lies above treeline. The tallest peak in the park is 14,255-foot Longs Peak, with its flat, football-field size summit.

A magical and rugged destination, it is here that fossil-laden bedrock emerged from ancient oceans. RMNP also encompasses several remaining glaciers. Below these snow and ice fields, most basins contain other glacial remnants—turquoise lakes that formed in moraines, those classic U-shaped valleys. An estimated 150 lakes are scattered throughout the park, some nestled high on remote shelves in the wilderness that remain frozen almost year-round. Other icy lakes occupy pastoral, forested settings, and are simply great hiking destinations.

RMNP is open year-round, with cross-country skiing and snowshoeing popular winter activities. Portions at higher elevations, including Trail Ridge Road and its Alpine Visitor Center, Moraine Park Museum, and the Lily Lake Visitor Center (as well as some ranger stations), close during the winter. The Beaver Meadows, Kawuneeche, and Fall River Visitors Centers are open all year, and can provide detailed maps and complete information on park regulations, current trail conditions, camping availability, fishing restrictions, accessibility for the disabled, and other important details to make your visit to the park safe and enjoyable.

The most ideal time for hiking in RMNP is between the months of June and October. That's the time when the park is most appealing—fields of colorful wildflowers enhance the high valleys while the skyscraping peaks still sparkle with snow, providing a spectacular backdrop—but also the most crowded. Approximately half of annual visitors come during the summer months; many simply to drive the summer-only Trail Ridge Road that connects the east edge of the park to its western side.

To help alleviate traffic congestion along Bear Lake Road, which leads to many of the most popular trailheads and campgrounds on the eastern half of the park, a free shuttle bus operates during the summer months. The parking area for the shuttle is located across from the Glacier Basin Campground.

The extensive park remains a place for explorers and adventurers to enjoy in an appreciative and responsible way. When visiting, respect the environment you are entering. It is your responsibility to help protect it from environmental damage. Tread lightly and stay on approved trails. If you trample a patch of sensitive alpine tundra with a careless step, it may take hundreds of years for the plants to recover.

Hikers may not bring their canine companions along with them on the trails. Dogs are not allowed outside of campgrounds, picnic areas, and along road shoulders anywhere in the park.

Portions of the park, including the easily accessible and paved Trail Ridge Road, reach elevations dangerous to visitors with any sort of physical impairment or those coming from lower elevations. It is important to be watchful of potential altitude sickness. Some people experience symptoms of altitude sickness—headache, nausea, dizziness, and difficulty breathing—at elevations as low as 6,000 feet. Descend to a lower elevation immediately should these symptoms set in.

Another safety consideration is to sign in on trailhead registration lists (when available) prior to beginning your hike. This gives park rangers an estimate of the number of people on the trails. As of January 2005, the entrance fee to RMNP is $20 for a seven-day pass or $35 for an annual pass. Overnight campground and backcountry camping permit fees are separate; for Summer 2004, the fees were $20 per night or backcountry trip.

Hiking at RMNP is immensely satisfying, but it is not without risk. Hike
wisely and be alert to your surroundings. Contact information for the park is
included in Appendix A on p. 261.

The following hikes are arranged
by point of origin, from north to south.
For example, from the Longs Peak
Trailhead, hikers can choose among
many destinations: Chasm Lake, Glacier
Basin, Battle Mountain, Longs Peak, and
Estes Cone. Some trails originate outside
the park boundaries; in those cases, complete driving directions to the trailhead
are given.

> "Of all the large and rugged mountain ranges in the world...[the Rockies] are the most friendly, the most hospitable."
>
> —Enos Mills

The trailheads listed in this guide are all accessible from entrances located
on the eastern edge of RMNP. The town of Estes Park contains many signs
pointing the way to the park, and the park maintains excellent signage pointing
the way to individual trailheads.

From Boulder, to reach:

The Fall River Entrance Station: Take US 36 north to Estes Park. At the stoplight,
go straight to get onto US 34. Follow this about 5 miles to RMNP. You will pass
the Visitor Center and shops before you reach the entrance station.

Beaver Meadows Entrance Station: Take US 36 north to Estes Park. At the stoplight, bear left to stay on US 36 and drive west about 3 miles to RMNP. The
Visitor Center is located near the entrance.

Lily Lake Visitor Center: Take US 36 north to Lyons. Turn left onto CO 7 rather
than turning right toward Estes Park. Follow CO 7 to Lily Lake. Turn right at the
Visitor Center, which is across the street from the lake.

Longs Peak Ranger Station: Take US 36 through Lyons. Turn left on CO 7 and
drive to Longs Peak Road, 2 miles north of Meeker Park. Turn left and drive
about 1 mile to the Longs Peak Ranger Station parking lot.

Wild Basin Entrance Station: Take US 36 north through Lyons. Turn left on
CO 7. Drive about 20 miles to the Wild Basin sign. Turn west and drive, about
1 mile to the Copeland Lake area. Follow the narrow gravel road to the Wild
Basin station.

Bridal Veil Falls

The 3-mile trip to Bridal Veil Falls is truly a place where dreams may lead you.

The trail begins at the Cow Creek Trailhead, along a decades-old gravel service road, passing the historic McGraw Ranch house and numerous cabins. The area was a working farm in the later part of the 1800s and restored into a dude ranch for vacationers in the early 1900s. Although the National Park Service has purchased the property, visitors should be mindful that portions of the area are still privately owned.

Today, scientists and researchers work in the area studying bear behaviors and butterfly habits, among other things.

From the trailhead, make your way behind these structures and past a few interesting interpretive signs, and you'll come to public facilities on your right. Begin your gradual ascent in the exposed meadow with intermittent spring and summer wildflowers and a few trees shading the trail.

Eventually the footpath narrows while it follows Cow Creek down and to your left. Cross over some log steps as you weave into a more forested area. Because of its lower elevation, the trail is often free of snow when trails elsewhere in the park are snow-covered.

Look for the famous Rabbit Ears to your left about 1.5 miles into the trip. You'll pass by Lumpy Ridge to the south (left) and Sheep Mountain to the north (right) as you make your way along. A spur to your left will take you to Gem Lake and the Twin Owls Trailhead (see Hike 50, p. 157).

Opposite: Bridal Veil Falls, Cow Creek, Bridal Veil Falls Trail, Rocky Mountain National Park

You'll cross Cow Creek several times on single-plank bridges. The final mile offers a steep ascent in the most shaded part of the path, which is unfortunate in the summer months. The stream bordering the trail rushes with small waterfalls.

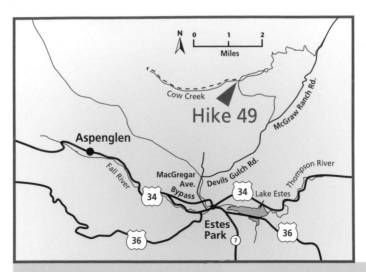

To the trailhead:	From Boulder take US 36 north to Estes Park. Drive through the stoplight past the Stanley Hotel. Turn right on MacGregor Ave. Follow the road as it becomes Devils Gulch Road. Turn left after 3.5 miles on McGraw Ranch Road to the Cow Creek Trailhead. Arrive early, as parking is very limited.
Distance:	6.6 miles round-trip
Difficulty:	Moderate
Elevation gain:	1,000 feet
Dogs:	No
Highlights:	No RMNP entrance fee; historic ranch and research facilities; newly built outhouse along trail; popular hike for dating couples
Jurisdiction:	Rocky Mountain National Park

The last pitch to Bridal Veil Falls is a rock scramble up a large rock slab just after you pass a corral and a sign indicating no horses beyond that point.

Climb briefly on that large rock and then look down and to your left for a small cairn, where the actual trail reemerges. Climb upward to the source of the smaller waterfalls. Bridal Veil Falls, while not spectacularly large, mists the air when winds blow through the boulders.

Gem Lake

Pine trees, Gem Lake, Gem Lake Trail,
Rocky Mountain National Park

Everyone I've ever spoken with adores Gem Lake. The hike lasts just an hour or so—the memories, much longer.

The sand and gravel trail leading to Gem Lake is an adventurous, yet well-traveled path leading to an icy and serene lake cradled by towering granite slabs. In a simple and unassuming way, tiny Gem Lake is without a doubt one of the most beautiful places in the world.

Beginning at an elevation of 7,740 feet, the short, steep trail gains 1,090 vertical feet in about 2 miles. The trail, lined with ponderosa pine, Douglas fir, aspen, and juniper, meanders through the aptly named Lumpy Ridge rock formations and affords intermittent scenic views of the Estes Park Valley.

Begin the outing in the conservation easement area of MacGregor Ranch, which has earned a designation on the National Register of Historic Places. Be mindful of the endearing billy goats lazing around the road as you make your way to the parking lot. Some days the goats are out, some days they are not.

The trail is to the east near the public facilities tucked away in the trees. Expect a gradual and steady ascent all the way to the lake along the easily identifiable trail. The route penetrates the aromatic pine-scented forest of eastern RMNP. Watch where you put your feet. I once saw a snake slither across the trail and I nearly lost my composure.

About 10 minutes into your hike you'll pass a fork on your left leading to the Bowels of the Owls, Upper Twin Owls, and Gollum's Arch climbing routes. Continue on the Gem Lake Trail, and you will soon come upon a large rock formation on your left dubbed Paul Bunyan's Boot. From here, the trail zigzags with a couple of switchbacks and leads directly to the lake.

Rocks and lichens, Gem Lake Trail, Rocky Mountain National Park

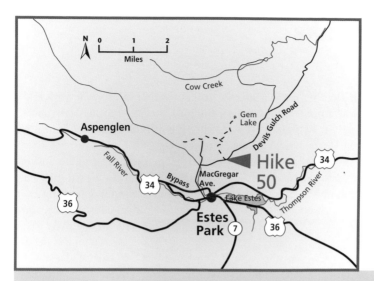

To the trailhead:	Take US 36 north to Estes Park. Drive through the light past the Stanley Hotel. Turn right (north) on MacGregor Ave. to MacGregor Ranch. Turn left (north) into the ranch and follow this narrow, paved road for 0.8 mile to the Twin Owls Trailhead. The Gem Lake Trail begins at the eastern end of the parking lot. The area is suitable for about 20 vehicles, and no parking is permitted along the 0.75 mile one-lane road leading to the parking lot.
Distance:	3.6 miles round-trip
Difficulty:	Easy to moderate
Elevation gain:	1,090 feet
Dogs:	No
Highlights:	No RMNP entrance fee; public facilities at trailhead; tiny lake framed by granite slabs; peculiar large boot-shaped boulder along the way
Jurisdiction:	Rocky Mountain National Park

You may also access Gem Lake via the Gem Lake Trailhead, located a few tenths of a mile past the entry to MacGregor Ranch on your left. This is a particularly good option if the Twin Owls Trailhead parking lot is at capacity. Hiking from the Gem Lake Trailhead extends your trek 0.2 mile to the lake.

Mountains

Lawn Lake

During their October mating season, bull elk gather in Moraine Park and bugle as they attempt to lure females. Bighorn sheep—the classic symbols of Rocky Mountain National Park—venture out at midday to the natural salt mineral lick in Horseshoe Park near Sheep Lakes.

Winter, spring, summer, or fall, the large open meadows of Horseshoe and Moraine Parks are two of the best places to hike and view wildlife. Park rangers and volunteers assist visitors with photo and viewing opportunities in an effort to least startle the animals.

The 6.2-mile trail to Lawn Lake starts in Horseshoe Park and heads north. This is a quiet, rarely traveled trail into the beautiful Mummy Range. The trail begins steeply into a series of switchbacks and presents the toughest part of the outing. A few minutes into your hike you will be walking right alongside Roaring River, adjacent to its steep banks.

Roaring River through rocky gorge, Lawn Lake Trail, Rocky Mountain National Park

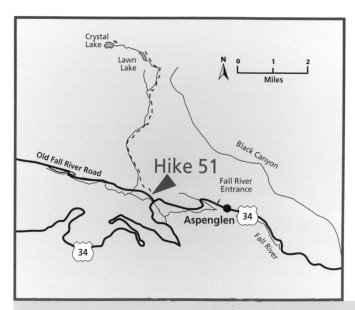

To the trailhead:	From the Fall River entrance (see p. 153), drive almost 2 miles, turning right on Old Fall River Road. The trailhead is 100 yards on your right.
Distance:	12.4 mile round-trip
Difficulty:	Moderate to strenuous
Elevation gain:	2,249 feet
Dogs:	No
Highlights:	Less-traveled trail; several picturesque lakes along the route
Jurisdiction:	Rocky Mountain National Park

Along a sandy area, the left (west) branch of the trail leads 3 miles to Ypsilon Lake. Stay right. As you continue to walk north, look down the sheer walls to the Roaring River and see uprooted and broken trees dislodged by the 1982 Long Lake Dam flood.

Eventually you'll enter the forest and climb three more switchbacks. When you reach another fork, veer left to stay on the Lawn Lake Trail, not right onto the Black Canyon Trail.

Soon you'll come to Lawn Lake, sitting high, cold, and glowing-clear at 10,789 feet, the lowest in a tier of pools that includes Crystal Lake.

Mountains

Cub Lake

Another great lake hike is the short trail leading to Cub Lake, nicely framed by the forests of the park.

To start the hike, cross a footbridge covering a swampy marsh just west of the Moraine Park Campground. As you continue along the trail, expect to cross two more bridges. You'll pass by water-loving shrubs and, depending on the time of year, various wildflowers. Cub Lake got its name for a reason, so keep a watch out for bears.

Soon, you'll enter a densely wooded section of the trail made up of ponderosa pine and Douglas fir. As the trail leads you along an incline, there are large boulders and exposed bedrock left from 13,000 or so years ago. From here, the trail descends to moister terrain and a meadow. Veer right at the trail junction, following the edge of the meadow toward the west. Right about here, the trail begins an ascent through aspens and offers a series of switchbacks before you reach Cub Lake. While steep in some areas, it's not too difficult.

The trail circling the shallow lake connects to a junction that leads to Mill Creek Basin. This short and easy hike is not a destination for anglers, as the tiny lake has no fish.

Water lilies, Cub Lake, Cub Lake Trail, Rocky Mountain National Park

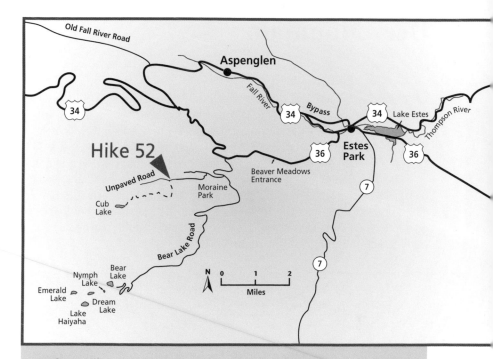

Old Fall River Road

Aspenglen

Fall River

34

34

Bypass

34 Lake Estes

Thompson River

Hike 52

Unpaved Road

36

Estes Park

36

Beaver Meadows Entrance

7

Cub Lake

Moraine Park

Bear Lake Road

Nymph Lake

Bear Lake

Emerald Lake

Dream Lake

Lake Haiyaha

7

N

0   1   2

Miles

To the trailhead:	From the Beaver Meadows Entrance Station (see p. 153), turn left and take Bear Lake Road 1.4 miles over a ridge to Moraine Park. Follow the road toward the campground and continue for 0.5 mile. Turn left and drive 2.2 miles to the Cub Lake Trailhead. Parking is limited and no parking is allowed roadside. Additional parking is available about 1 mile farther up the road at the Fern Lake Trailhead.
Distance:	4.6 miles round-trip
Difficulty:	Easy
Elevation gain:	540 feet
Dogs:	No
Highlights:	Short trail along intermittent lush wetlands; ideal outing for kids
Jurisdiction:	Rocky Mountain National Park

Deer Mountain

One not-too-difficult hike in RMNP is the 1,083-foot climb up Deer Mountain. Three miles one-way, the footpath isn't terribly steep but the views from its 10,013-foot summit are virtually unsurpassed anywhere else in the park.

To begin the hike, go east uphill for a steady zigzagging incline with Ypsilon Mountain (part of the Mummy Range) coming into view eventually.

The first 2 miles are steeper than the final stretch, but not at all difficult. Be sure to not leave the trail and do not walk left toward the rock outcroppings, because that is not the way to the summit. The trail levels out for the final mile, then veers sharply right (south) to the top. You'll soon come upon a trail marker indicating that the summit is to your right.

Penstemon, lower slopes of Deer Mountain, Rocky Mountain National Park

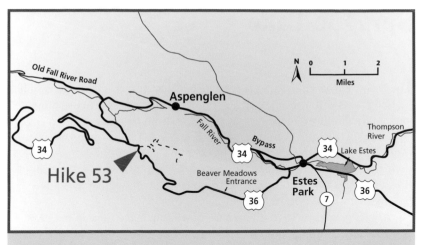

To the trailhead:	From the Beaver Meadows Entrance Station (see p. 153) stay right and follow US 36 about 2.9 miles northwest to where it meets US 34. The Deer Mountain Junction Trailhead is on your right. Park along the road.
Distance:	6 miles round-trip
Difficulty:	Easy to moderate
Elevation gain:	1,083 feet
Dogs:	No
Highlights:	Wide-open views of the Estes Park Valley from the broad summit; seen from elsewhere in the park, Deer Mountain looks square, like a box
Jurisdiction:	Rocky Mountain National Park

A steep, but brief, rock-stepping ascent leads the way to the summit. From the top of Deer Mountain, distant peaks loom in all directions. Sharp-eyed visitors with binoculars can usually spy elk, bighorn sheep, and other wildlife traversing the meadows and crags. Look down to the Beaver Meadows Entrance Station and beyond to the entire Estes Park Valley.

This is a really satisfying hike to do with teenagers.

Sprague Lake

The beauty of the short Sprague Lake loop is that it is wheelchair-accessible, enabling folks with special needs to enjoy the wilderness. Furthermore, some of the best views in the park can be see from the lake's eastern edge.

Sprague Lake sits at an elevation of 8,710 feet. The Sprague Lake Nature Trail Loop circling the icy water is made up of boardwalk and gravel all along its relatively flat surface. The lake is framed by stands of towering pine, offering shady picnic areas. It is also a fine fishing hole for native greenback cutthroat trout.

As elsewhere in RMNP, all manner of wildlife make their home near Sprague Lake. Depending on luck and the time of day, you may see a rabbit, raccoon, grouse, porcupine, weasel, mountain lion, fox, coyote, elk, deer, bear, cougar, owl, or even an eagle.

Otis and Hallett Peaks and Flattop Mountain, Sprague Lake at dawn, Rocky Mountain National Park

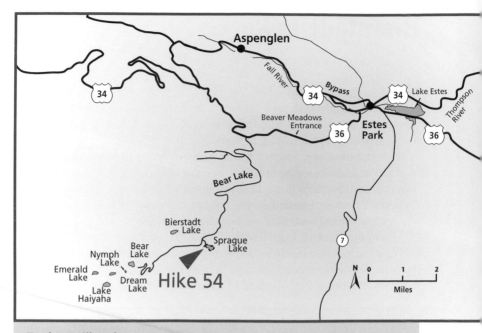

To the trailhead:	From the Beaver Meadows Entrance Station (see p. 153), take the first left on Bear Lake Road and continue to the Sprague Lake turnoff on your left.
Distance:	1-mile loop
Difficulty:	Easy
Elevation gain:	Negligible
Dogs:	No
Highlights:	Wheelchair-accessible nature trail; fishing permitted (state license required)
Jurisdiction:	Rocky Mountain National Park

If it's inspiration and solitude you seek on a warm day, this probably isn't the most ideal lake to visit at RMNP. However, this high-country jewel is a favorite destination for many, located just inside the park along Bear Lake Road.

Mountains

Bierstadt Lake

Hiking in the fall is sometimes the best time to get out—the air is chilly with its invigorating nip and the colors are brilliant. A crisp wind rattled through the forest and we could see our breath the early morning we hiked the short, forested trail leading to Bierstadt Lake.

The not-too-steep, 1.5-mile trail leading to the high-mountain lake is ideal for out-of-town visitors who are in reasonably good condition yet may be unaccustomed to the altitude. Bring plenty of water, because the trail can be dry and occasionally exposed during hot summer days. Some trees along the way offer refreshing and much-welcome spots of shade.

From the Bierstadt Lake Trailhead, the path toward the high lake zigzags back and forth along a gentle incline across Bierstadt Moraine. The trail initially starts in a dense evergreen forest and then intermittently opens up to provide magnificent views of the surrounding mountains as it works its way up.

Otis and Hallett Peaks and Flattop Mountain reflected in Bierstadt Lake, Rocky Mountain National Park

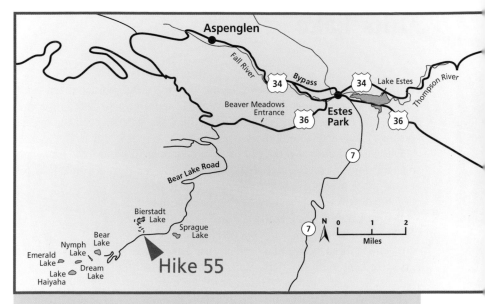

Aspenglen

Fall River

34   Bypass   34   Lake Estes

Thompson River

Beaver Meadows
Entrance

36   **Estes
Park**   36

7

Bear Lake Road

Bierstadt
Lake

Sprague
Lake

Bear
Lake

Nymph Lake

Emerald Lake

Lake
Haiyaha

Dream
Lake

7   N   0   1   2

Miles

Hike 55

To the trailhead:	From the Beaver Meadows Entrance Station (see p. 153), take the first left on Bear Lake Road and continue for 6.5 miles to the Bierstadt Lake Trailhead on the right. During the months when the shuttle bus is in service, park in the shuttle bus parking lot and take the bus to the trailhead.
Distance:	2.8 miles round-trip
Difficulty:	Easy to moderate
Elevation gain:	566 feet
Dogs:	No
Highlights:	Good lake hike for people coming from out of state or much lower elevations
Jurisdiction:	Rocky Mountain National Park

Closer to the lake, the footpath levels off and you are surrounded by a pine-scented, forested area of spruce, aspen, and even lodgepole pine. Bierstadt Lake, which lies on your right (northeast), is accessible from a small path. If you miss this side trail, there are numerous well-marked junctions around this area, so simply follow the trail markers to Bierstadt Lake.

The gnarled, knotted trail surrounding the lake is damp and seemingly mysterious. If you opt to walk around the lake on the mile-long flat footpath, you'll be provided spectacular views. From a little beyond the lake, you can see Longs Peak and Glacier Gorge.

Mills Lake

Most visitors to the park come to see the towering rocky peaks, but expending a little effort to find a tucked-away lake is definitely worth the time and energy. And the pleasant little outing to Mills Lake satisfies even the most seasoned backpackers and hikers.

At just 2.5 miles from the Glacier Gorge Junction Trailhead, the lake offers an opportunity for spectacular photographs. Some even consider Mills Lake to be one of the prettiest lakes in the park, and it also offers an incredible lakeside view of stunning Spearhead, a 1,000-foot granite prism rising skyward.

Opposite: Mills Lake and Keyboard of the Winds, Rocky Mountain National Park

To get to the lake, begin at the Glacier Gorge Junction Trailhead located at a bend on Bear Lake Road. Access the trail south to Alberta Falls. Follow this wide trail past fern and aspen as it climbs gently 0.6 mile to the stunning falls. Take a right turn at two forks along the footpath.

The route continues to parallel Glacier Creek deeper into the forest, passing rock formations and spruce and fir woodlands. The footpath twists its way on the rocky trail and granite outcroppings, as the views become more dramatic. On your way, look for the huge Glacier Knobs formation to the right.

Mills Lake, Rocky Mountain National Park

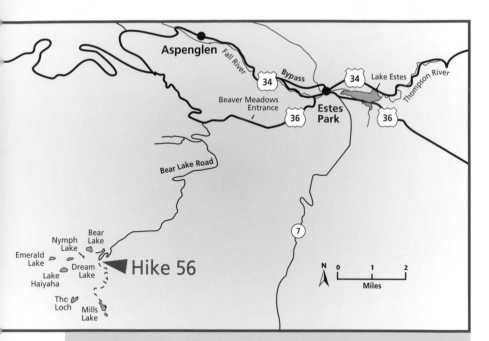

Aspenglen

34 Bypass 34 Lake Estes

Beaver Meadows Entrance

36 Estes Park 36

Bear Lake Road

Bear Lake
Nymph Lake
Emerald Lake
Dream Lake
Lake Haiyaha
The Loch
Mills Lake

7

Hike 56

N 0   1   2
        Miles

To the trailhead:	From the Beaver Meadows Entrance Station (see p. 153), take a left on Bear Lake Road and drive to the shuttle bus parking area. Take the bus to the Glacier Gorge Junction Trailhead. In seasons when the bus is not in service, continue on Bear Lake Road to the trailhead.
Distance:	5 miles round-trip
Difficulty:	Easy to moderate
Elevation gain:	700 feet
Dogs:	No
Highlights:	Lake named for Enos Mills, one of the founders of RMNP; fishing permitted (state license required)
Jurisdiction:	Rocky Mountain National Park

Alongside massive glacial boulders, the trail increases in steepness for about 1 mile to the lake. This final stretch is not unmanageable and not too taxing.

Shining Mills Lake, named for Enos Mills, a man who worked tirelessly to establish the park, is situated at 9,940 feet above sea level and is stocked with rainbow trout.

Ribbon Falls

Ribbon Falls, near Black Lake, Glacier
Gorge Trail, Rocky Mountain National Park

Mountains

The southbound trail to Ribbon Falls leads you into a remarkable glacial landscape valley.

Starting at an elevation of about 9,300 feet at the Glacier Gorge Trailhead, the trail penetrates the gorge past Alberta Falls and Glacier Falls. Subalpine forest fringes undeniably pretty Mills Lake (See Hike 56, p. 170), 2.5 miles farther along the way to Ribbon Falls.

You could stop your hike at Mills Lake and enjoy a picnic lunch, completing the round-trip outing of a noteworthy total of 5 miles. Some people do choose to hike this far, mainly to fish. If you disagree with Mark Twain that, "There is no use walking five miles to fish when you can depend on being just as unsuccessful near home," push on. You won't be disappointed.

Next you'll pass tiny Jewel Lake, just south of Mills Lake almost immediately on your right.

The trail continues through woodlands with scattered spring and summer wildflowers and alternating moist bogs. Finally, following the unmistakable, hard-to-lose trail you'll come to your destination.

Suitably named Ribbon Falls, its 140-foot tumbling ribbon of white water rushes down a monolith of polished granite. At the falls, you will have traveled just over a formidable 4.5 miles, paralleling Glacier Creek the entire way.

Glacier Creek below Ribbon Falls, Rocky Mountain National Park

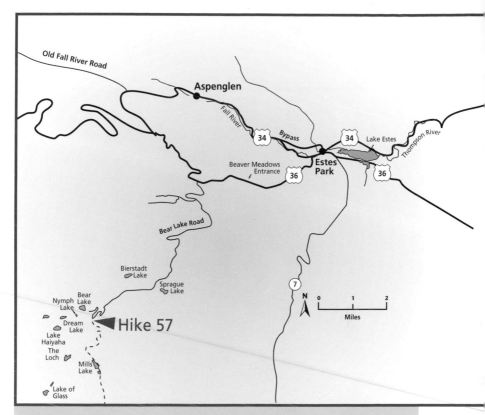

Old Fall River Road

Aspenglen

Fall River

34 Bypass 34 Lake Estes

Thompson River

Beaver Meadows
Entrance 36 Estes Park 36

Bear Lake Road

Bierstadt Lake

Sprague Lake

7

N 0 1 2

Miles

Bear Lake
Nymph Lake

Dream Lake

Lake Haiyaha

The Loch

Mills Lake

Lake of Glass

◀ **Hike 57**

To the trailhead:	From the Beaver Meadows Entrance Station (see p. 153), take a left on Bear Lake Road and follow the signs to the shuttle bus parking area. Take the bus to the Glacier Gorge Junction Trailhead. In seasons when the bus is not in service, continue on Bear Lake Road to the trailhead.
Distance:	9.6 miles round-trip
Difficulty:	Moderate to strenuous because of distance
Elevation gain:	1,330 feet
Dogs:	No
Highlights:	Like a running water faucet, the slender falls tumble 140 feet; lengthy, worthwhile outing
Jurisdiction:	Rocky Mountain National Park

Black Lake

Alberta Falls, near Glacier Gorge junction, Rocky Mountain National Park

On some hikes, you can turn back anywhere along the way and still call it a success. However, the farther into RMNP you hike, the better it seems to get.

And nowhere is that more evident than on the trails originating in and around Glacier Gorge Junction. Hikers can opt to trek only as far as nearby Alberta Falls, Glacier Falls, or Mills Lake; press farther on to spectacular Ribbon Falls or trek all the way to the end of the trail at Black Lake.

The 4.7-mile trail leading to Black Lake veers south through high-country forests and exposed, often windy, meadows. Gaining about 1,400 feet of elevation in not quite 5 miles, the outing to tiny Black Lake isn't for the half-hearted. But the reward—scenery almost too beautiful to believe—is your incentive.

To begin the trek, take the shuttle bus to the Glacier Gorge Junction Trailhead. Follow the trailhead signs along the Glacier Gorge Trail as it contours around to the southeast, crossing a creek on a bridge.

Staying on the trail, you'll eventually reach Alberta Falls and soon a turnoff on your left to the North Longs Peak Trail (see Hike 68, p. 201). But stay on the Glacier Gorge Trail and you'll come to another turnoff on your right to Lake Haiyaha. Continue south (going left) and you will pass Mills Lake and, just 0.2 mile from Black Lake, Ribbon Falls. Continue to Black Lake. If time and weather permit, have lunch and then turn around and return the way you came.

McHenrys and Arrowhead Peaks, Black Lake, Rocky Mountain National Park

To the trailhead:	From the Beaver Meadows Entrance Station (see p. 153), turn left on Bear Lake Road and follow the signs to the shuttle bus parking area. Take the bus to the Glacier Gorge Junction Trailhead. In seasons when the bus is not in service, continue on Bear Lake Road to the trailhead.
Distance:	8 miles round-trip
Difficulty:	Moderate to strenuous because of distance
Elevation gain:	1,400 feet
Dogs:	No
Highlights:	Hike takes the greater part of a morning; numerous appealing offshoots along the way
Jurisdiction:	Rocky Mountain National Park

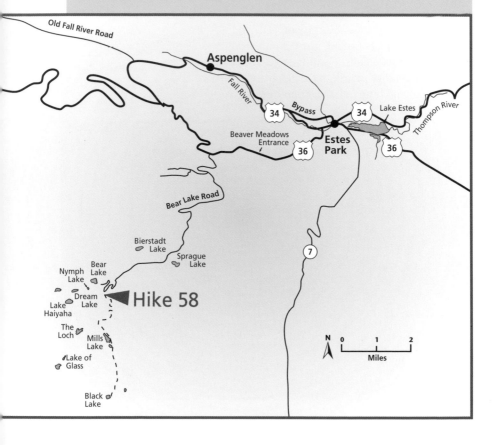

Sky Pond

Quiet Sky Pond is a sparkling mountain lake cradled in a lofty cirque. The view all along the way leading to Sky Pond is surreal in its beauty.

The new Glacier Gorge Trailhead, accessible via shuttle bus, is a sylvan area, fern-lined and shaded with aspen. As you make your way along the 4.9-mile trail to Sky Pond, you'll pass the Lake of Glass. Don't expect it to glisten like a sheet of glass, however. It shimmers and ripples most of the time because of gusty, high winds.

From the trailhead, Glacier Gorge Trail leads you past the 25-foot rushing cascade of Alberta Falls. Take the right-hand fork weaving through quiet meadows of seasonal wildflowers in the Loch Vale Valley and then the left-hand fork just before scrambling up a rocky hillside near Timberline Falls.

Beyond the Lake of Glass (called Glass Lake by the U.S. Board of Geographic Names), Sky Pond can be a bit tricky to find. Veer right from Glass Lake and look for cairns above you perched on boulders.

Expect one small stretch of actual rock climbing, which isn't technical. After that, it is a walk south along the western edge of the Lake of Glass.

A near postcard-perfect setting, Sky Pond glows turquoise-green. Looking up from the small lake, you'll see the east face of 13,153-foot Taylor Peak and Taylor Glacier.

What you don't want to miss while you're at Sky Pond are the craggy dramatic spires along the lake's shoreline. From here you can see Sharkstooth Peak, Loch Vale Pinnacle, Sabre, Cathedral Spires, and the needle of Petit Grepon. If you time your outing just right, you may encounter a few technical rock climbers crawling up the spires like Spidermen.

Looking down on Lake of Glass, Sky Pond Trail, Glacier Gorge area

Mountains

To the trailhead:	From the Beaver Meadows Entrance Station (see p. 153), turn left on Bear Lake Road and follow the signs to the shuttle bus parking area. Take the bus to Glacier Gorge Junction Trailhead. If the shuttle bus is not in service, continue on Bear Lake Road to the trailhead on your right.
Distance:	10.8 miles round-trip
Difficulty:	Moderately strenuous because of distance
Elevation gain:	1,800 feet
Dogs:	No
Highlights:	High mountain pond; little-traveled route
Jurisdiction:	Rocky Mountain National Park

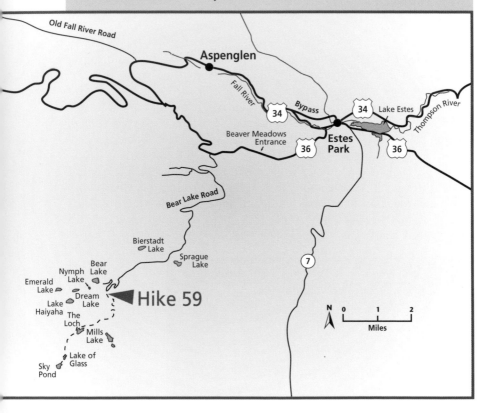

Emerald Lake via Bear, Nymph, and Dream Lakes

The hike to Emerald Lake takes you past Bear, Nymph, and Dream Lakes, and climbs just 605 feet through wooded terrain.

Because of the ease of the hike, the trail to Emerald Lake is ideal for hikers of nearly all ages and abilities. Dream Lake, at 1.1 miles, is thought to be the most photographed lake in the park, especially since it marks a good turn-around point for many hikers, particularly those with small children.

The Bear Lake Trailhead is at the end of Bear Lake Road. This is a busy trail. If you can get away to do the hike on a weekday, you may encounter fewer hikers and more solitude.

Start your trip to Emerald Lake by passing Bear Lake. My husband and I have hosted more than a dozen foreign exchange students from all over the world, and our sightseeing outings have nearly always included a trip to at least Bear Lake. This charming lake is circled by a paved 0.6-mile interpretive nature trail. Take the trail south into the forest and pass by tiny, tiny Nymph Lake at 0.5 mile. Snap a few photos or just continue on another 0.5 mile

Tyndall Gorge below Hallett Peak, east of Emerald Lake, Bear Lake area

to picturesque Dream Lake. Most visitors coming from sea level don't find the trip to Dream Lake too difficult.

As you follow the footpath to Emerald Lake, the route climbs 250 feet before reaching the eastern edge of the fourth lake. Views really open up along this section of the trail, revealing the stunning geology that makes up the park.

Species of trout found in a number of mountain streams and lakes include German brown, rainbow, brook, and cutthroat, and fishing is permitted in three of the four lakes on this hike. Because of the cold water at the higher altitudes, the fish do not grow very large.

To the trailhead:	From the Beaver Meadows Entrance Station (see p. 153), take a left and follow Bear Lake Road to where it dead-ends at the parking lot. During the months when the shuttle bus is in service, park in the shuttle bus parking lot and take the bus to the trailhead.
Distance:	3.6 miles round-trip
Difficulty:	Easy to moderate
Elevation gain:	605 feet
Dogs:	No
Highlights:	No fishing at Bear Lake; fishing permitted at Nymph, Dream, and Emerald Lakes (state license required); interpretive nature trail at Bear Lake
Jurisdiction:	Rocky Mountain National Park

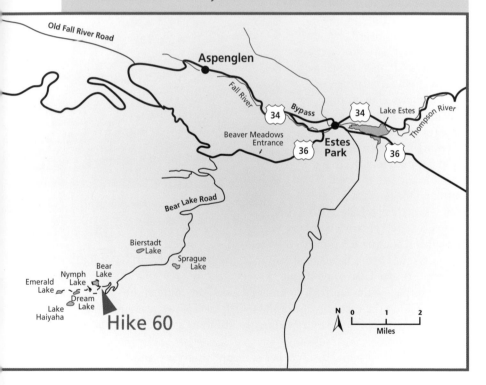

Flattop Mountain and Hallett Peak

One particularly good way to view the rugged beauty of the spectacular park is a hike to the 12,324-foot summit of Flattop Mountain.

Once at the top, marmots and Rocky Mountain bighorn sheep reign the above-timberline climes. Curious marmots scurry around the large boulder field amongst the alpine tundra hoping for lunch crumbs while the bighorns keep their distance. On your way to and from Flattop's summit, keep an eye out for deer, elk, eagles, and black bears.

If you opt to hike the mountain in the fall, you'll be treated to the vibrant aspens changing color and bright autumn ground cover. Once when I hiked up this trail, there was a herd of elk feeding in the meadows along the roadside. Some of the most often seen and photographed of Colorado's big game,

Photo by Bette Erickson

Flattop Mountain summit, Rocky Mountain National Park

Mountains

Flattop Mountain, from Glacier Gorge Trail, Glacier Gorge area

elk herds frequently wander along the road and even into the nearby town of Estes Park.

To start the hike, veer right on the trail circling Bear Lake rather than going left on the trail leading to Emerald Lake (see Hike 60, p. 181). Soon you'll take another right along the northern side of tiny Bear Lake.

Linking up to the long and well-defined footpath, expect a steady climb as markers point the way to Flattop Mountain. Take a left at the junction another 0.5 mile up the trail. Be sure not to turn right because that would take you to Bierstadt Lake (see Hike 55, p. 168).

In another 0.5 mile or so is your final intersection. Again, take the left fork. The trail on the right takes you to Odessa and Fern Lakes (see Hike 63, p. 189). From this junction it's about 3.2 miles to Flattop's summit.

The first part of your hike is in a densely forested area and if you're like me, you might appreciate the shade. Views really open up, however, once you reach timberline at about 11,400 feet, but the intense heat from the sunlight on a clear day also becomes apparent. You cannot lose the trail at this point, so continue on, and drink plenty of water to stay hydrated.

Aptly named, the summit of Flattop Mountain is broad and virtually level, a good place to kick back and enjoy the panorama. At this point, you've accomplished an invigorating 4.4-mile hike.

To the trailhead:	From the Beaver Meadows Entrance Station (see p. 153), turn left on Bear Lake Road, parking at the shuttle bus parking area. If the shuttle bus is not in service, continue on to the Bear Lake Trailhead at the end of Bear Lake Road.
Distance:	8.8 miles round-trip
Difficulty:	Moderate
Elevation gain:	2,849 feet
Dogs:	No
Highlights:	Hallett Peak is RMNP's mountain with the distinctive profile; the Flattop Mountain summit is unbelievably flat
Jurisdiction:	Rocky Mountain National Park

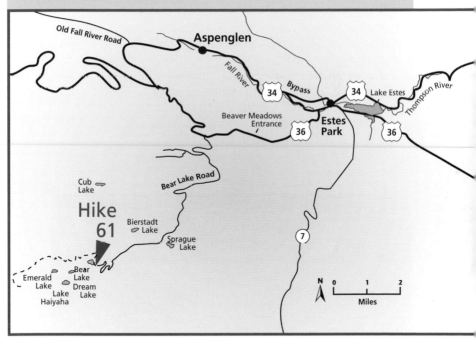

After a short rest and a snack (if time and weather permit), push on. The way to reach Hallett Peak is to veer left (south) and climb across the tundra at the head of Tyndall Glacier. Soon you'll be scrambling over boulders for only about 389 feet on a short, steep route to the 12,713-foot summit of Hallett Peak.

Mill Creek Basin via Hollowell Park

Surrounded by majestic mountains and accented by stands of fluttering aspen, the Mill Creek Basin Trail is a remarkable place to hike, particularly during middle to late September or early October. Autumn's bliss, with its peak of fall colors and golden aspen trees, neighboring the dark greens of spruce, fir, and pine, offers a welcome blend of vibrant contrasts. Indeed, Mill Creek Basin is one of my favorite fall hiking destinations.

To start the short hike, you'll park at Hollowell Park off of Bear Lake Road. Look for the large Mill Creek Basin Trailhead sign near clean public facilities.

After passing by the trailhead sign, you'll enter a spacious meadow framed by soaring mountains.

Continue along the single-track dirt trail that leads into a forested area. The climb is gentle and easy. During the fall, ankle-high purple asters are in bloom along the trail.

You'll be hiking right alongside churning Mill Creek. Listen to the rush and hum of the clear and cold mountain water along the 2.5-mile trail leading up to the Upper Mill Creek Basin Campground. Throughout the treelined footpath are several well-built log bridges.

Opposite: Aspen and spruce forest, Mill Creek Basin Trail, Hollowell Park area

Mill Creek, Mill Creek Trail, Hollowell Park area

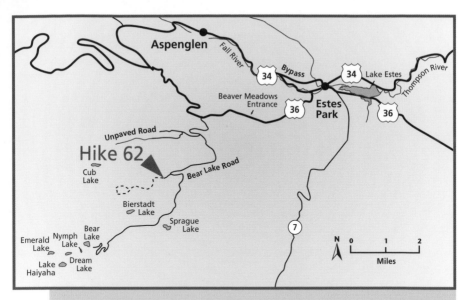

To the trailhead:	From the Beaver Meadows Entrance Station (see p. 153), take a left on Bear Lake Road and park at the Mill Creek Basin Trailhead in Hollowell Park on your right. During the months when the shuttle bus is in service, park in the shuttle bus parking lot and take the bus to the trailhead.
Distance:	5-mile loop
Difficulty:	Easy
Elevation gain:	600 feet
Dogs:	No
Highlights:	Very moderate climb; picturesque valley; public facilities at trailhead
Jurisdiction:	Rocky Mountain National Park

The final bridge is simply a two-plank crossover leading into the densely wooded campground. Cutting through the campground will loop you back around into Hollowell Park. However, taking a turnoff to your left, rather than going right to the campground, would direct you toward Bierstadt Lake (see Hike 55, p. 168). This area has plenty of directional signs, so if you're paying attention you shouldn't get lost.

One option is to extend your hike up to Bierstadt Lake, then exit via the Bear Lake Trail and catch the free shuttle bus at Bear Lake back to Hollowell Park.

Moraine Park to Fern Lake

Moraine Park's 245 campsites make it the park's largest campground, and it is open all year long. What's more, the hiking trails originating from Moraine Park are first rate. If you've ever considered camping the night before hiking, this is a good place to do it.

In addition to all the other choices of trails weaving through Moraine Park, the route to Fern Lake offers a variety of scenic pleasures and an impressive workout, making it a family favorite of ours. Starting at a trailhead elevation of 8,155 feet, you ascend a manageable 1,375 feet on a moderate 3.8-mile trail.

As you begin your outing, the first glorious encounter is The Pool at about 1.7 miles from the trailhead. At this point, you will have climbed an easy 245 feet. Perhaps it has seemed like a pretty average trail so far, but when you get to The Pool, it may delight and surprise you. A large pool of water surrounded by steep rock walls, The Pool is a part of the Big Thompson River.

Continue on across a large wooden bridge. Past this bridge the trail divides. Take the right (south) branch, going straight to Fern Falls, rather than veering left (north) to Cub Lake. The trail to the falls circles around south-facing slopes and climbs along the side of a gully, entering woodlands.

You can hear the roaring falls before you see the tumbling, icy water. By now you will have walked about 2.5 miles toward your target. Enjoy steep Fern Falls amid a jumble of downed timber. When the winds blow, a refreshing mist welcomes you.

Next it's on to Fern Lake, where the trail gets a bit steeper for 1 mile or so, but not at all difficult. A short segue south and west 1 mile from Fern Lake is Odessa Lake. Alternatively, just 0.8 mile to the west on a rarely traveled route is Spruce Lake. Cairns mark your way.

Fern Lake, Rocky Mountain National Park

To the trailhead:	From the Beaver Meadows Entrance Station (see p. 153), turn left and drive south on Bear Lake Road. At the Moraine Park Museum (open seasonally), take a right and drive due west about 1 mile up the valley to the trailhead.
Distance:	7.6 miles round-trip
Difficulty:	Moderate
Elevation gain:	1,375 feet
Dogs:	No
Highlights:	Secluded lake in high meadow; a variety of scenic pleasures along the route
Jurisdiction:	Rocky Mountain National Park

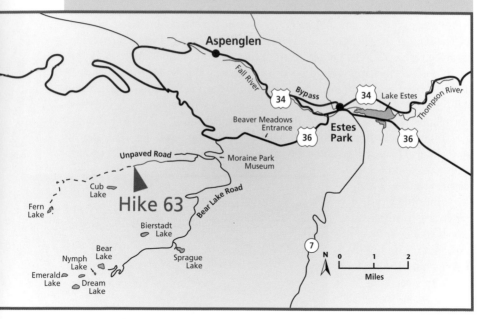

If you have more energy and USGS quad maps, keep going. From Spruce Lake, some ambitious hikers continue on along Spruce Canyon to 12,922-foot Stones Peak. You can also reach faraway Rainbow Lake, the eighth highest lake in RMNP. This route gains 3,585 feet in 7 miles. Be careful, though. The course is dangerously marshy, requiring precision with USGS quad maps and some technical climbing.

Lily Lake

Beguiling mallard ducks swim idly at Lily Lake. The less common ringneck ducks, too, can be seen diving into and gliding on the glistening lake, just south of Estes Park in the Tahosa Valley. Elk and deer refresh themselves in the water, too.

Bull elk, Lily Lake, Rocky Mountain National Park

Trout remain the mainstay of Colorado's $1.3 billion fishing economy, and abundant greenback cutthroats take the bait for anglers at Lily Lake. Fishing and sightseeing aren't the only reasons to visit the teeny lake, however.

To the trailhead:	Across from Lily Lake Visitor Center (see p. 153). Parking is plentiful.
Distance:	0.5-mile loop around the lake
Difficulty:	Easy
Elevation gain:	Negligible
Dogs:	No
Highlights:	Wheelchair accessible; fishing permitted (state license required); nearby Visitor Center; public facilities
Jurisdiction:	Rocky Mountain National Park

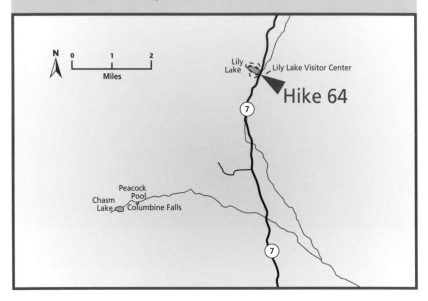

The wheelchair-accessible 0.5 mile trail circling the entire lake can be covered in about 20 minutes or so. You'll want to take your time to see all there is to see: the varied collection of trailside wooded plants and the elk-chewed quaking aspens as well as those special ducks.

The quiet lake shore is at 8,927 feet and the short detour trail climbs sharply up 9,786-foot Lily Mountain, directly to the north.

An excellent spot for a picnic on your way to or from Estes Park, the lake is frequented by friendly whistle pigs (yellow-bellied marmot) looking for handouts. But like elsewhere, please don't feed the wildlife.

Twin Sisters Peaks

Two nonprofits, the Conservation Fund and the Rocky Mountain National Park Associates, in 1990 solicited donations to buy private land along CO 7 near Lily Lake, between Allenspark and Estes Park. Soon after, they established the Lily Lake Visitors Center near the Twin Sisters Peaks Trailhead, a worthwhile stop following your hike.

Located beside the eastern edge of RMNP, the trail offers dozens of switchbacks adding interest and breaking up the monotony of the route leading to the two summits of Twin Sisters Peaks. Starting at an elevation of 9,000 feet, the trail weaves in and out of National Park lands as it winds south, then east to a windy 11,248-foot western summit.

Twin Sisters Peaks, Rocky Mountain
National Park

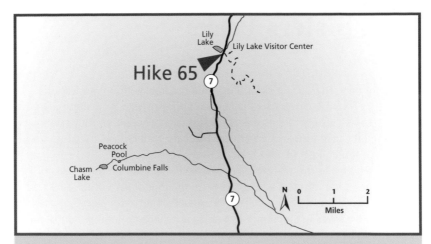

Hike 65

Lily Lake
Lily Lake Visitor Center

Peacock Pool
Chasm Lake — Columbine Falls

N   0   1   2
              Miles

To the trailhead:	The short gravel road from the Lily Lake Visitor Center (see p. 153) dead-ends at the trailhead.
Distance:	7.4 miles round-trip
Difficulty:	Moderate
Elevation gain:	2,428 feet
Dogs:	No
Highlights:	Numerous switchbacks; wildlife almost always spotted; public facilities at nearby Visitor Center
Jurisdiction:	Rocky Mountain National Park

A thick lodgepole pine forest shades a steep incline along the length of the zigzagging 3.7-mile trail. Lodgepole pines are prolific along the lower part of this trail because a fire destroyed a denser forest several years ago.

A stone hut and radio tower signify the western summit of Twin Sisters Peaks. Its neighboring peak to the east is just 15 feet higher and a short hike up along a large stone field. On a clear day from the summits, expect views of the Mummy Range to the north and across the Tahosa Valley, Longs Peak, and Mount Meeker further to the west.

Rocky Mountain bighorn sheep quietly promenade above treeline, and the morning we visited Twin Sisters Peaks was no exception. My hiking partners and I stopped and marveled at the five or so intriguing, curl-horned animals basking on the sun-drenched rocks. We were not the only awestruck hikers stopping and snapping photographs of this quintessential symbol of Western wilderness. And the family of buff-brown sheep seemed to oblige, rarely bothering to look up while nibbling the tundra edges.

Estes Cone

Isabella Bird, an English world traveler, left a classic account of 1870s Colorado: *A Lady's Life in the Rocky Mountains.* Bird writes that while she didn't particularly like most of the state, she fell in love with the Estes Park Valley and Longs Peak—both of which can be seen from the summit of Estes Cone.

Estes Cone north
summit, Rocky
Mountain National Park

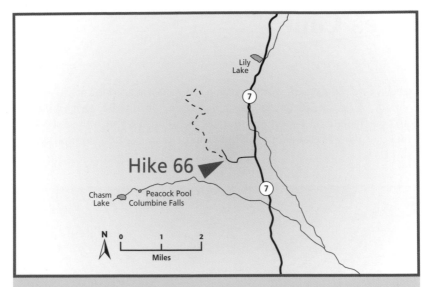

To the trailhead:	Start at the Longs Peak trailhead at the Longs Peak Ranger Station (see p. 153).
Distance:	6.5 miles round-trip
Difficulty:	Moderate
Elevation gain:	1,606 feet
Dogs:	No
Highlights:	Old mining ruins; sign-in canister buried in rocks at the summit; seen from some spots along CO 7, Estes Cone looks like a pyramid
Jurisdiction:	Rocky Mountain National Park

Hiking through a wooded forest on the Estes Cone Trail takes you past the remains of Eugenia Mine and on to panoramic views of Longs Peak and Mount Meeker, Lumpy Ridge, the Mummy Range, and the Estes Park Valley.

The Eugenia Mine—about 1.5 miles into the hike and off to the left of the trail—was worked by the Norwell family and last filed a silver claim in 1919. Historical records indicate that the family owned a piano at this homestead located at 9,908 feet—presumably hauled up by mule.

To start the hike, begin at the Longs Peak Trailhead and sign in at the trail register. This trailhead is one of only a very few that offer a trailhead registration sign-in notebook.

Follow the Longs Peak Trail but leave the footpath and turn right at the junction indicating the way to Eugenia Mine and Storm Pass.

At about 2 miles into the hike, you'll come to a spacious meadow called Moore Park. This area offers a wonderful view of the Twin Sisters Peaks (see Hike 65, p. 193) and an up-close and rocky profile of Estes Cone.

The Storm Pass Trail weaves north all the way to its trailhead off of Bear Lake Road. Eventually, though, you'll want to leave Storm Pass at 10,250 feet and turn right (east) to reach the 11,000-foot Estes Cone. As you come to a rock field, just follow the cairns that point the way to the summit. While at the top, be sure to locate the peak sign-in register, a canister nestled in the boulders at the highest point of the mountain.

Eugenia Mine site, Estes Cone Trail, Rocky Mountain National Park

Chasm Lake

At 11,760 feet above sea level, stunning Chasm Lake is tucked below Longs Peak's imposing east face. Dubbed "The Diamond," the jutting east-facing granite slab rises an additional 2,000 feet above the lake, and is an impressive, even dizzying, sight seen from the lake.

Chasm Lake is best viewed and photographed during the mid-morning, with the sunlight and shadows aligned just right. That means, however, leaving the Longs Peak Ranger Station Trailhead very early in the morning to make the moderate 4.2-mile trek.

If you're up to leaving the trailhead even earlier, a pre-dawn arrival at the lake provides some glorious alpenglow photographs. Of course, arriving that early would also avoid the crowds that seek out the popular lake, particularly during summer weekends.

Some seasons, because of late snowfall, the trail is not navigable even into July. So call ahead to inquire about trail conditions. (Contact information is in Appendix A on page 261.)

The first half of the trek rambles through moderately steep lodgepole pine and aspen groves, with a few steep switchbacks. You'll pass by gurgling Alpine Brook and through Goblins Forest. (I've not yet seen any Goblins while strolling through that densely forested terrain, although I've been on the lookout.)

The wide, well-used Longs Peak Trail (see Hike 68, p. 201) snakes through the trees before breaking out into a broad basin. The Chasm Lake Trail forks left at about 3 miles instead of going right to access Longs Peak. Take the left branch, passing a turnoff to Columbine Falls, Peacock Pool, and the flanks of Mount Lady Washington to the north (on your right) and Mount Meeker to the south (on your left).

Right about at this junction, the view of the Roaring Forks drainage is literally almost too beautiful to describe. A break for photos at this point is necessary. Watch out for snow on the trail, and use caution when walking across snow banks. A small slip could yield a dangerous fall toppling on the rocks many feet below.

Opposite: Ships Prow, east face of Longs Peak, Chasm Lake Trail

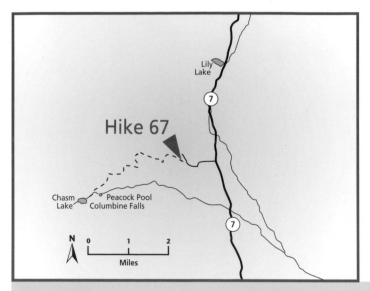

To the trailhead:	Start at the Longs Peak Trailhead at the Longs Peak Ranger Station (see p. 153).
Distance:	8.4 miles round-trip
Difficulty:	Moderate
Elevation gain:	2,360 feet
Dogs:	No
Highlights:	The Diamond granite slab towers above the lake; sights all along the way make this hike meaningful
Jurisdiction:	Rocky Mountain National Park

You'll soon pass a Park Service storage hut used to house rescue equipment and supplies, locked when not in use. Continue on, as the lake is just a short scramble away through the krummholz, those short and twisted trees stunted by strong winds and thin air.

The lake itself, at a depth of approximately 100 feet, is fishless, probably because of the icy water at that altitude. While at the lake, look up toward The Diamond. You may see a daring climber or two scaling the rock wall. A pair of binoculars in your backpack will come in handy.

Longs Peak

Aspen trees in fall, east face of Longs
Peak, Rocky Mountain National Park

Climb if you will, but remember that courage and strength are nought without prudence, and that a momentary negligence may destroy the happiness of a lifetime," climber Edward Whymper advised. If you're looking for a heart-pounding ascent along steep rock walls, step through the Keyhole on the Longs Peak Trail.

This is a hike of extremes. To be certain, there's no boredom on the long, 7.5-mile Longs Peak Trail leading to its 14,255-foot summit. One of the six mountains making up the Front Range fourteeners, Longs Peak attracts thousands of visitors each year. For hikers with a full day on their hands seeking a vigorous workout, this is the right hike. The first 6 miles are a gentle, moderate climb. However, because of the difficulty of the last 1.5 miles, it's not the most suitable fourteener to climb for first-time peak baggers.

Trekking at a moderate pace, expect to reach the summit in about 6 hours. For this reason, leave the trailhead well before dawn and try to get off the summit by noon. Sadly, numerous people have died on Longs Peak because of falling or being caught in afternoon electrical storms.

From the Longs Peak Trailhead, follow the well-marked East Longs Peak Trail. The beginning hike along the flank of the mountain is gentle, open, and pleasant. A stroll through its Goblins Forest is enchanting.

Be careful not to veer off the trail at several junctions: Keep left at the Eugenia Mine-Storm Pass junction and left at the Jims Grove intersection. Take the right-hand fork and do not detour to Chasm Lake (see Hike 67, p. 198).

At about 6 miles from the trailhead, at 12,750 feet, you will come upon an expansive boulder field. Above the rocks, just below the Keyhole, is a stone shelter built in memory of a hiker who died on the mountain.

At 13,150 feet, the Keyhole is an interesting, craggy rock outcropping stretching northward. Stepping through the Keyhole, expect a precipitous rock pitch with incredible views. It is here that nature mocks you, even as it takes your breath away.

It is okay to rest, have a snack, take some incredible pictures, and turn around at this point. Many find climbing this route along the steep rock wall, marked only by painted yellow-and-red bull's eyes, too unsettling. Trust your instincts, noting sweaty palms and heightened anxiety. Prudence demands attention.

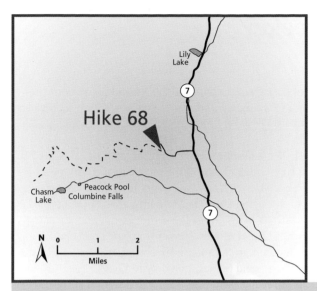

To the trailhead:	Start at the Longs Peak Trailhead at the Longs Peak Ranger Station (for directions see p. 153).
Distance:	15 miles round-trip
Difficulty:	Strenuous
Elevation gain:	4,855 feet
Dogs:	No
Highlights:	Large, flat football-size summit; beguiling stone hut at boulder field
Jurisdiction:	Rocky Mountain National Park

If you still have energy, and you are up for an adrenaline rush, hiking past the Keyhole will serve you well. If you do proceed, follow the bull's eyes toward the summit's cliffs leading up a series of steep ledges; a large couloir called the Trough; an exposed protrusion known as the Narrows; and along the Homestretch. A long, steep, smooth slab of granite, The Homestretch takes you 100 or so feet to the summit.

Time and weather permitting, take a break at the summit and reward yourself with a snack and a couple of photos before heading back carefully the way you came.

Mount Meeker

Not in the clamour of the street, not in the shouts and plaudits of the throng, but in ourselves, are triumph and defeat," wrote poet Henry Wadsworth Longfellow. Reaching the top of Mount Meeker is a good place to find peace and learn your strength.

Mount Meeker looks like a fourteener, but in reality it's not. This spectacular mountain, with its spiny ridge, is one of the most conspicuous mountains along the Front Range, its south and east slopes towering over north Boulder and visible from throughout the Denver metro area. Some people confuse Mount Meeker with its twin, Longs Peak.

Most hikers access 13,911-foot Mount Meeker from the Longs Peak Trailhead. A less-traveled mountain than its sister, Mount Meeker is often disregarded, but in RMNP, it is secor ' 'n elevation only to Longs.

To start the hike, begin ʳ ˌy early (say, 4 a.m.) and sign in at the ranger's station kiosk at ʻ ˌrailhead. Follow the well-marked Longs Peak Trail and be sure to ˌy left at the Eugenia Mine-Storm Pass junction, about 0.5 mile into vˮ ˌike.

Agaiɲ ˌer left 2.5 miles along the trail at the Jims Grove junction. You'll come ˈ ˌne Chasm Lake connection at 3.5 miles. Here you'll leave the Longs Pˮ ˌ Trail and hike southwest (left) along the Chasm Lake Trail (see Hike 67, p. 198) for 1 mile to Chasm Meadows at 11,580 feet. A solitary stone cabin sits in Chasm Meadows.

Chasm Lake is at 11,800 feet above and to your west, but stay on the trail and go south toward Meeker's north side. From here, walk south along a stream coming to a prominent rock wall dubbed the Ships Prow.

At about 12,000 feet, go left (east), hiking along a large talus field. Do not segue up unto the cliffs along Mount Meeker's north face. Soon you'll come to what's called the Loft, a broad saddle between Longs and Meeker. Watch for cairns to help direct your way.

Opposite: Mount Meeker and Peacock Pool, Chasm Lake Trail, Rocky Mountain National Park

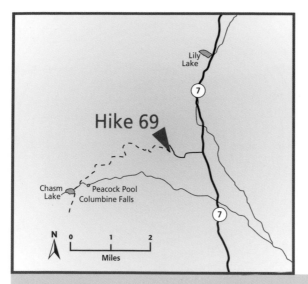

Hike 69

To the trailhead:	Start at the Longs Peak Trailhead at the Longs Peak Ranger Station (see p. 153).
Distance:	12 miles round-trip
Difficulty:	Strenuous
Elevation gain:	4,591 feet
Dogs:	No
Highlights:	Half of Twin Peaks (Longs Peak and Mount Meeker) visible from Boulder; trip takes the better part of a day
Jurisdiction:	Rocky Mountain National Park

Follow the faint trail south to Meeker's northeast ridge at 12,900 feet. Hike 0.6 mile southwest up the ridge on large talus blocks. From here it's a pretty steep rock scramble west to the summit.

Longs Peak stands tall to the north and west, with Pagoda Mountain south of Longs. Watch out for high winds on the exposed slopes, and expect views of serenity from the top. Have a well-deserved snack (chocolate, anyone?), take some photos, and return the way you came.

Wild Basin Area including Ouzel Falls, Calypso Cascades, and Bluebird Lake

During the cold and snowy months, the Wild Basin Area is a quintessential winter wonderland. It is a cross-country skier's and snowshoer's dream. It's not to be passed up during the warmer months, either. The Wild Basin Area, whether you choose to ski it or hike it, is one of most popular backcountry stops east of the Continental Divide.

Calypso Cascade,
Bluebird Lake Trail,
Wild Basin area

Numerous appealing trails originate here. Besides being surrounded by dense, sweet-scented forests, what makes the Wild Basin Area so truly special is the opportunity to create your own hike with numerous permutations. The aromatic scent of pine and earth, among other sensory pleasures, await you when you push yourself along the lengthy trail leading to fishless Bluebird Lake, passing so many interesting landmarks along the way.

The Bluebird Lake Trail weaves through cozy forests and meadows past Copeland Falls, Calypso Cascades, Ouzel Falls, and Ouzel Lake ending at Bluebird Lake. Stunning Calypso Cascades is a mere 1.8 miles from the trailhead while the 12,716-foot Ouzel Peak stands tall at more than 6 miles in, just south and west beyond the Bluebird Lake Trail. Many hikers don't go the entire way to the lake because of the numerous appealing stopping-and-turning-around points along the trail.

In the shadow of Ouzel Peak and Copeland Mountain, at 10,978 feet, the rocky shore of Bluebird Lake is a coveted destination because of the privacy the lake provides to those who endure the steep ascent.

The route is well-marked with several wooden bridges crisscrossing over St. Vrain Creek. As you hike further along a steep and steady incline, the area opens up to reveal a high mountain valley.

Do not veer right on the Thunder Lake Trail about 1 mile after you pass Copeland Falls. Stay on the trail to access stunning Calypso Cascades. At

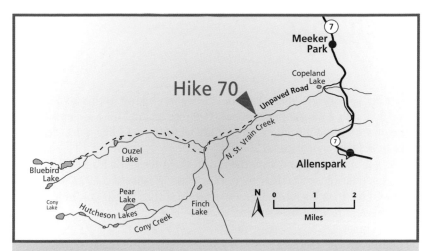

To the trailhead:	Start at the Wild Basin Entrance Station (see p. 153).
Distance:	12.4 miles round-trip
Difficulty:	Strenuous
Elevation gain:	2,478 feet
Dogs:	No
Highlights:	Wild Basin Entrance Station typically closes the second weekend in October, so entrance after that date is free; during the summer season, the entry fee is $20 for a seven-day pass, $35 for an annual pass
Jurisdiction:	Rocky Mountain National Park

Calypso Cascades there is a trail junction. Stay right, as the trail on your left is the Allenspark Trail to Finch Lake (see Hike 71, p. 210).

Ouzel Falls is the next stop as you hike north and west. Views of Mount Meeker and Longs Peak are to the north. Climbing several switchbacks and crossing over a couple of bridges, the trail circles below the ridge from which Ouzel Fall drops.

At the final trail junction, go left and climb steeply south to the crest of a moraine. At 1.3 miles from that trail junction is the spur to Ouzel Lake. The trail rambles along rocks and back through trees, and into a meadow again, ending at Bluebird Lake, about 1.4 miles farther.

Opposite: Ouzel Falls, Bluebird Lake Trail, Wild Basin area

Finch Lake

Whether you spell it Allens Park or Allenspark, hiking in this area is pretty much always a pleasant experience. If you're looking for a sweet hike, this is it. An outing to remote Finch Lake feeds the soul like a decadent piece of Belgian chocolate.

As you make your way into the forest, the Allenspark Trail eventually opens up, offering spectacular mountain views because of a 1978 forest fire. Improved habitats for mule deer are a result of that fire. If you're lucky, you may see a few. Be sure to keep your eye out for the gentle creatures and walk quietly.

Although you can access Finch Lake from the Wild Basin Trailhead (see Hike 70, p. 207), starting from Allenspark offers a more direct route, less befuddling to hikers, with fewer twists, turns, and connections.

The beginning of the trek offers a steep climb up a wooded drainage and meets with aptly named Confusion Junction at about 1.5 miles in. From this intersection, continue south and west as the trail levels off for 2.3 miles to Finch Lake.

Shoreline grasses, Finch Lake, Wild Basin area

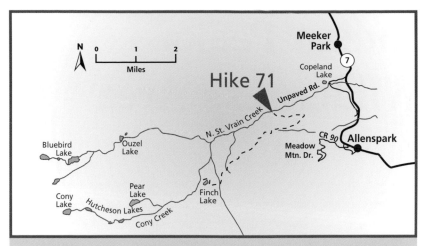

To the trailhead:	From Boulder, head north on US 36 to Lyons. Take CO 7 toward Allenspark. At the stop sign by the post office, take CR 90 straight uphill (it becomes Skinner Road) to Meadow Mountain Dr. Turn right and the Allenspark Trailhead is on your right.
Distance:	6.2 miles round-trip
Difficulty:	Easy to moderate
Elevation gain:	1,000 feet
Dogs:	No
Highlights:	Little-traveled trail to quiet, photogenic lake
Jurisdiction:	Rocky Mountain National Park

Actually, the last 0.5 mile or so is a descent down to the lake, crossing several small streams. Finch Lake, at 9,912 feet, is calm and serene, reflecting Copeland Mountain on a clear day. The best photo opportunities exist from the eastern shore of the lake.

If you're ambitious and so inclined, the trail circling the lake on the north side leads 2 miles uphill steeply before reaching Pear Lake. From Pear Lake, you can see Ouzel Peak in its dramatic splendor to the west.

Mountains

Indian Peaks
Wilderness Area

When even the remotest reaches of Rocky Mountain National Park seem too populated, a hike through pristine wilderness can be a refreshing change. It can also be more challenging, and hikers are cautioned to be well-prepared for any eventuality when venturing far from civilization into the backcountry.

What distinguishes a designated "wilderness" from a national park or forest? A dedicated wilderness area is a place where the imprint of the human race is substantially unnoticed, and regulations and ethics are in place to help it remain that way. There are no roads, for instance, in a wilderness area, while at times there are even traffic jams in national parks. Trailhead parking, you'll notice, is located well outside of wilderness boundaries. Wilderness areas are under the jurisdiction of the U.S. Forest Service, as are national forests, while the U.S. Department of the Interior is responsible for operating the national parks.

The U.S. Congress passed the Wilderness Act in 1964, restricting grazing, mining, and mechanized vehicles or equipment in selected wilderness areas. The lands are protected and valued for their experiential, ecological, historical, and scientific resources. Located in the Arapaho and the Roosevelt National Forests, Colorado's Indian Peaks Wilderness Area (IPWA) was recognized by Congress and added to the National Wilderness Preservation System in 1978.

This wilderness landscape covers nearly 76,000 acres, following the Continental Divide south for some 16 miles, and contains 35 named peaks, many named for Indian tribes and chiefs of the West. Rocky Mountain National Park borders its northern edge.

Millions of years ago, the saw-toothed summits of the IPWA were shaped by the grinding action of glaciers. IPWA still contains numerous cirque basins with several remnant glaciers, the southernmost lasting glaciers in North America. Below these snow and ice fields, most valleys contain other glacial remnants—turquoise lakes that formed in moraines—among acres of fragile alpine tundra.

There are about 50 lakes here, 41 of them named. Streams in the wilderness include South and Middle St. Vrain, Boulder, Buchanan, Cascade, and Arapaho creeks. Most of the waters sustain populations of assorted species of trout, including native cutthroat and rainbow, brook, and brown trout. A Colorado state fishing license is required for all anglers over the age of 16.

Wildlife consists of elk, large-eared mule deer, mountain lions, black bears, bobcat, ptarmigan, and snowshoe hare.

With more than 130 miles of hiking routes and convenient trailhead access available, IPWA gets much foot traffic. In fact, the area is the most frequently visited wilderness in the Rocky Mountain states.

When hiking in IPWA, remember that whatever you carry into the wilderness, you must carry out. That means that nothing should be left or buried in the backcountry, including picnic supplies or food scraps. I'm not at all opposed to picking up a discarded apple core, for instance, left by a careless hiker. Many of us find joy in leaving the wilderness seemingly untouched.

While Ralph Waldo Emerson's advice, "Do not go where the path may lead, go instead where there is no path and leave a trail," may be fitting for your career goals, it is not an idea to embrace while in the backcountry. Stay on designated trails and avoid bushwhacking through the forests and off trail, here and elsewhere. Walk single file, where necessary. Keep in mind that what took nature thousands of years

> **"I find that in contemplating the natural world my pleasure is greater if there are not too many others contemplating it with me, at the same time."**
>
> **—Edward Abbey**

to create can be destroyed by one careless hiker within a matter of minutes. Please be attentive and careful to keep the wilderness wild.

Dogs must be leashed at all times for good reason: Leashed dogs offer less chance of conflict with wildlife. In addition, leashed dogs provide a more enjoyable experience for other hikers. (Believe it or not, some people may not want to be eagerly greeted by your affectionate dog.)

Backcountry permits are required to camp anywhere inside the wilderness boundaries. Contact the Boulder Ranger District of the Arapaho and Roosevelt National Forests for information. (Contact information is in Appendix A on page 260.)

As well-traveled as the IPWA has become, solitude can still be found in some places throughout its vast landscape, particularly on weekdays. The Indian Peaks Wilderness Area is truly one of Colorado's crown jewels.

The following dozen or so trails, while they originate at different locations, penetrate IPWA, taking you deep into nature. They are organized according to point of origin.

Indian Peaks Wilderness Area

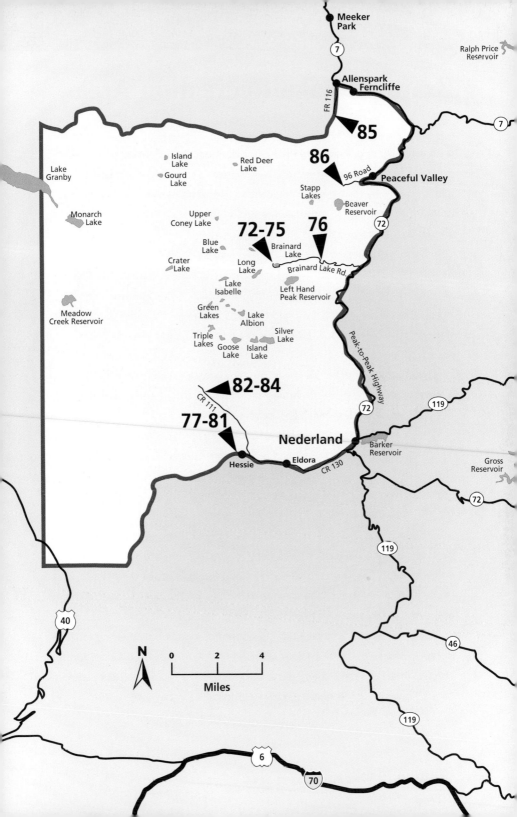

Brainard Lake Recreation Area

The Brainard Lake Recreation Area, located just east of IPWA, is the focal point for many hiking destinations. Often, hikers stay at the well-developed and always lively campground adjacent to the lake the night before. At the time of this printing, an entrance fee of $6 for a five-day pass or $25 for an annual pass is charged for driving in here.

Gleaming Brainard Lake sits at an elevation of 10,345 feet. Historians believe the lake is named for Colonel Wesley Brainard, a prospector who developed numerous claims during the late 1800s. The paved road circling the lake is one-way to the right and crosses a bridge at the outlet. Directional signs help guide your way along this road to the Long Lake and Mitchell Lake Trailheads.

Nearly every summer weekend the region bustles with hikers. Be mindful, however, that many of the destinations originating from Brainard Lake are still blanketed with fresh snowfall as late as into June.

The paved road to Brainard Lake is closed from late October through late June or July. A temporary trailhead is accessible outside the locked gate for cross-country skiers and snowshoers wanting to explore the area. An interesting and invigorating winter outing is the roughly 8-mile loop originating from the entrance gate at the Red Rock Trailhead.

To reach Brainard Lake Recreation Area from Boulder, you have two options, both scenic drives. Take Lefthand Canyon west 12 miles to Ward. Take an immediate left (west) on Brainard Lake Road (CR 102) off of the Peak-to-Peak Highway (CO 72). Travel approximately 5 miles on the paved road to the Brainard Lake Entrance Station.

Another option is to take CO 119 up Boulder Canyon to the tiny town of Nederland. Take the Peak-to-Peak Highway (CO 72) north from Nederland for about 8 miles to Ward. Turn west on Brainard Lake Road (CR 102) and drive about 5 miles to the Brainard Lake Recreation Area.

Jean Lunning Scenic Trail

A short nature walk looping around Long Lake from Brainard Lake gains only about 200 feet in elevation in an easy 2.5 miles or so along the Jean Lunning Scenic Trail.

Access this trail at the Long Lake Trailhead. The trail veers to the left at the lower end of Long Lake, whereas the Pawnee Pass Trail goes right. The Jean Lunning Trail merges again with the Pawnee Pass Trail at the upper end of Long Lake. Views throughout the area include the craggy and often

Indian Peaks, Jean Lunning Trail,
Brainard Lake area

Indian Peaks Wilderness Area

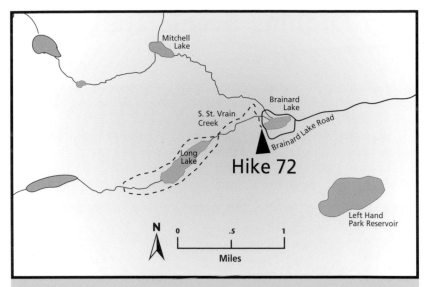

To the trailhead:	The Long Lake Trailhead is 0.5 up the left fork of a side road that turns off at the west end of the lake (for directions see p. 216).
Distance:	Varies
Difficulty:	Easy to moderate
Elevation gain:	Varies
Dogs:	Yes, on leash at all times
Highlights:	Ideal for older adults and families with young children; picnicking opportunities throughout the area
Jurisdiction:	Boulder Ranger District, Arapaho and Roosevelt National Forests

snowcapped summits of the Indian Peaks and the surrounding coniferous forest with its soothing shades of green. Because of the ease and convenience of the Jean Lunning Trail, many visitors bring along picnic supplies, blankets, and chairs. And don't forget your camera.

The Colorado Mountain Club has placed trail markers along the CMC South, Waldrop, and South St. Vrain Trails for a slightly longer hike looping around Brainard Lake. This route gains about 400 vertical feet.

Lake Isabelle

Indian Peaks, above Lake Isabelle, Brainard Lake area

While some lower-elevation hikes lose their wildflowers by late June, the higher elevations are often still bursting with color. If you're searching for a bit of untamed wilderness, sprinkled with vivid, seasonal flowers, a trip to Lake Isabelle may be for you.

Although the Pawnee Pass Trail leading to the lake can be crowded with foot traffic on weekends, you can still expect some peaceful moments of solitude at the lake and along the winding trail.

Begin the hike at the Long Lake Trailhead. Access the Pawnee Pass Trail as it heads west into the thick, quiet forest of Engelmann spruce and subalpine fir. The vegetation along this route flourishes because of the relative humidity. This subalpine zone—from 9,000 feet to about 11,500 feet—gets more moisture than other areas in Colorado. Snow stays on the ground longer in the shaded woodland, thus keeping the area moist further into the following warmer and dryer season.

The first part of the trail starts at 10,500 feet above sea level and climbs gradually the entire way to Lake Isabelle. You can expect no trail junctions or complicated unmarked intersections.

Navajo Peak and Navajo snowfield, Pawnee Pass Trail above Lake Isabelle

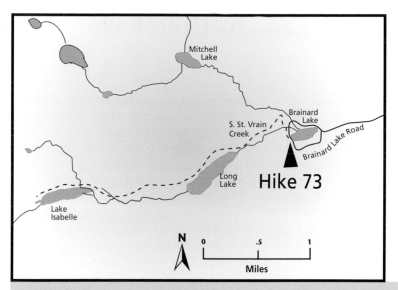

Mitchell
Lake

Brainard
Lake

S. St. Vrain
Creek

Brainard Lake Road

Long
Lake

Hike 73

Lake
Isabelle

N

0   .5   1

Miles

To the trailhead:	Follow the signs around Brainard Lake to the Long Lake parking area at the west end. (For directions, see p. 216)
Distance:	4.2 miles round-trip
Difficulty:	Easy
Elevation gain:	368 feet
Dogs:	Yes, on leash at all times
Highlights:	Great outing for people new to hiking; fishing permitted (state license required)
Jurisdiction:	Boulder Ranger District, Arapaho and Roosevelt National Forests

The trip really is a straightforward nature walk. As the spongy footpath ascends the forested valley through the meadow splashed with wildflower color, particularly in June and July, be mindful of the whole community of fauna found in the forest: Insects, mammals, and birds make their home here. Tread carefully.

At about 2 miles in, or 30 minutes, depending on your pace, veer left (south) to Lake Isabelle. Not only is the trip here one of the easiest and most pleasant trails in the IPWA, Lake Isabelle has the added benefit of being stocked with rainbow trout.

Mitchell Lake to Blue Lake

A hike to Blue Lake revels in alpine mountainscape beauty. Winding and climbing from Brainard Lake through a dense forest, you'll come upon spectacular vistas en route to the base of 12,979-foot Mount Toll.

After hiking briefly from the Mitchell Creek Trailhead and crossing a bridge over Mitchell Creek, you'll enter the actual wilderness boundary. The first 0.5 mile or so of the trail is flat and wide. A brief segue takes you to Mitchell Lake at 10,700 feet.

At this point, the footpath becomes a bit steeper but never too exhausting. Press on to Blue Lake as the trail crosses a wide stream on a wooden bridge. Finally, you'll arrive at a rocky area and possibly snowfields (depending on the season), where the trail comes close to timberline. Walk carefully, being sure to stay on designated trails.

Trail to Mitchell and Blue Lakes

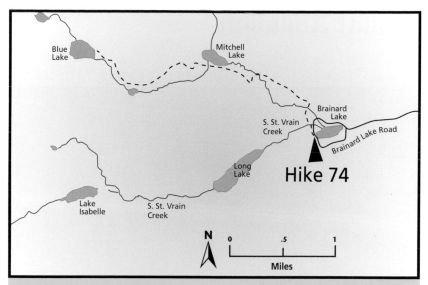

To the trailhead:	Follow the signs around Brainard Lake to the Mitchell Lake parking area at the west end (for directions, see p. 216).
Distance:	5 miles round-trip
Difficulty:	Moderate
Elevation gain:	840 feet
Dogs:	Yes, on leash at all times
Highlights:	Mount Toll looks like a pyramid towering over Blue Lake; fishing permitted (state license required)
Jurisdiction:	Boulder Ranger District, Arapaho and Roosevelt National Forests

Blue Lake lies in a rock cirque at 11,352 feet above sea level. Rugged Mount Toll dominates the skyline with its prominent pyramid shape. From here you can also see Pawnee Peak and Paiute Peak. About half of the Blue Lake shoreline is accessible for fishing. The 23-acre lake is stocked with cutthroat trout.

Indian Peaks Wilderness Area

Mount Audubon

Mount Audubon reflected in Brainard Lake, Brainard Lake area

Named for the famous naturalist and painter, Mount Audubon offers views to rival those from any fourteener located in the state.

Start your hike at the Beaver Creek Trailhead on the north side of the Mitchell Lake parking area. Walk through a pine-scented coniferous forest for a brief time before reaching timberline in just about 1.5 miles.

The Beaver Creek Trail continues on toward Coney Flats. Here at the saddle is a view down into the Coney Lake drainage area. With just a couple of switchbacks and steep areas, the Mount Audubon Trail continues to climb gently among the talus.

During the early season, a snowfield may still be lingering, blocking the trail near the end. Cairns are strategically placed, marking the trail leading directly to the summit toward your left (west).

The peak itself is spacious with several waist-high, manmade windbreak shelters in which to take a rest and perhaps enjoy lunch before heading back down the way you came.

Mount Audubon and the Indian Peaks reflected in Red Rock Lake, Brainard Lake area

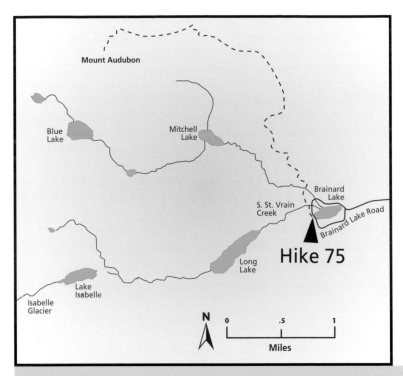

Blue Lake

Mount Audubon

Mitchell Lake

Brainard Lake

S. St. Vrain Creek

Brainard Lake Road

Hike 75

Long Lake

Lake Isabelle

Isabelle Glacier

N

0   .5   1

Miles

To the trailhead:	Follow the signs around Brainard Lake to the Mitchell Lake parking area at the west end (for directions, see p. 216).
Distance:	8 miles round-trip
Difficulty:	Moderate
Elevation gain:	2,740 feet
Dogs:	Yes, on leash at all times
Highlights:	One of the most rugged and scenic hikes originating from the Brainard Lake area; easily identifiable trail
Jurisdiction:	Boulder Ranger District, Arapaho and Roosevelt

Although you can hike Mount Audubon year-round, the paved road to Brainard Lake is closed from late October through late June or July. So be aware that if you visit during that time you will need to add 5 miles onto the length of your trip, parking outside of the locked gate.

Sourdough Trail

Mitchell Creek, near Sourdough Trail, Brainard Lake area

Indian Peaks Wilderness Area

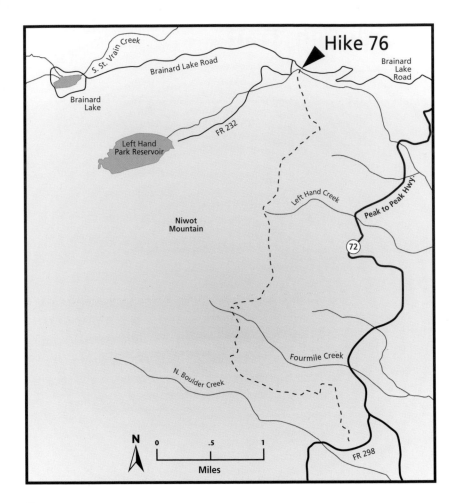

Hike 76

S. St. Vrain Creek

Brainard Lake Road

Brainard Lake Road

Brainard Lake

FR 232

Left Hand Park Reservoir

Left Hand Creek

Peak to Peak Hwy

Niwot Mountain

72

Fourmile Creek

N. Boulder Creek

N

0   .5   1

Miles

FR 298

Since the 1800s, people have flocked to Colorado first for the mining and then for the reputed healing effects of our dry climate. Nowadays, many people come for hiking and other outdoor sports. A visit to the Sourdough Trail may not yield strikes of gold or silver, but it almost always promises therapeutic effects as a result of getting away and feeling new again.

Don't be fooled, though: This is a long trail, stretching about 14 miles from its northern end at Peaceful Valley to its southern end near the University of Colorado Mountain Research Station. My favorite portion is at the middle section going south along Niwot Mountain's east ridge, through forests and along several creek drainages ultimately ending at Sourdough Trail's farthest southern end.

To the trailhead:	Follow the directions to Brainard Lake. (For directions, see p. 216.) The trailhead will be on your left before you reach the entrance station. Park along the road where permitted.
Distance:	11.6 miles round-trip from the north Red Rock Trailhead going south to the Sourdough Trailhead off of Rainbow Lakes Road.
Difficulty:	Moderate to strenuous because of the length of the round-trip outing.
Elevation gain:	1,000 feet
Dogs:	Yes, on leash at all times.
Highlights:	Gradual, very sustained elevation gain; pleasantly wooded trail
Jurisdiction:	Boulder Ranger District, Arapaho and Roosevelt National Forests

To begin the hike, park along Brainard Lake Road where permitted outside of the entrance station. Tiny Red Rock Lake is close to this trailhead, just west of the entrance station south of Brainard Lake Road. The Sourdough Trail is a sought-after seasonal destination for cross-country skiers and snowshoers in winter, and mountain bikers during warmer weather.

The wooded footpath climbs gently. It ascends a small ridge, closely paralleling Niwot Ridge Road, and then loops around southward. Along the way, you'll climb to the trail's highest spot just before Fourmile Creek. Eventually you'll cross the creek on a wide bridge.

The southernmost Sourdough Trailhead at 5.8 miles into the trip is a good place to rest, have lunch, and turn around—unless you've made arrangements to do a car swap at each end of the trail or you have much more energy and time to spare. Directly west of this trailhead is the University of Colorado Mountain Research Station.

The Sourdough Trail stretches 8.9 miles farther north of the Red Rock Trailhead, weaving its way through forests, past Beaver Reservoir, all the way to the Buchanan Pass Trailhead at Peaceful Valley (see Hike 86, p. 256.)

If you don't want to park near the Brainard Lake entrance station, you can access the Sourdough Trail at its southern end. To do this, drive from Boulder on CO 119 to Nederland. Take the Peak-to-Peak Highway (CO 72) north 7 miles, then turn west on unpaved Rainbow Lakes Road (CR 116). The trailhead parking is 0.4 mile on the left and the trail is on the right. There are many more parking spaces at this location and public facilities are available.

Hessie Townsite

Gold and silver mining was prevalent in the Colorado high country during the mid to late 1800s, particularly around Lost Lake and Jasper Creek, west of Eldora. Captain J.H. Davis established a thriving mining camp in the area and named it after his wife, Hessie. Hundreds of people once lived and worked here. That was more than a century ago. Now the Hessie Townsite is quiet except for a few cabins and mining ruins scattered here and there. Much of the land is privately owned, so be courteous to residents.

The trails weaving and intersecting throughout the Hessie area offer some of the best hiking near Boulder. The stretch of road to the actual trailhead is a cobblestone creek bed and may be waterlogged well into June, so high clearance vehicles are recommended.

If you choose not to drive that last portion, a footpath to your right in the forest parallels the road and the walk to the trailhead isn't far at all, about 0.25 mile. This path is located just down and to the right of the turnoff to the Fourth of July Campground (see Hikes 82–84, p. 245). Continue walking on this trail for less than 20 minutes or so as views really open up and you'll have reached the actual Hessie Trailhead parking area.

Visitors to the Hessie Townsite may want to know that winter here is an increasingly popular season, too, with numerous opportunities for snow-shoeing, cross-country skiing, and wildlife viewing.

To reach Hessie from Boulder, take CO 119 to Nederland. At the south end of Nederland, take a right on CR 130 and travel 0.5 mile to the town of Eldora. Stay right instead of going to Eldora Ski Area. Continue on Eldorado Avenue as far as you can. Drive slowly past Eldora about 1.5 miles to the sign on your left indicating Hessie Townsite.

Lost Lake

The forest lies open and pine needles carpet the ground. The trees combined with grasses and shrubs offer a palette of color year-round along the trail to Lost Lake. Clear mountain air frames snowcapped, glacier-carved peaks, cutting a jagged line against the sky in the Indian Peaks Wilderness Area.

The trek to Lost Lake is along an easy trail leading to the 9,786-foot lake. It is canopied with towering, fragrant evergreens. Hikers and non-hikers throughout the area routinely marvel at the forest's poetic wilderness topography. This was always a favorite spot of mine to take our two young children or friends from out of town. No surprise either: Lost Lake really isn't lost at all.

Cow parsnip, Lost Lake, Hessie
Townsite area

Indian Peaks Wilderness Area

From the Hessie Trailhead, walk west over a bridge crossing Middle Boulder Creek's North Fork and into the forest. Look for a large trailhead kiosk with maps of the various trails available: King Lake, Woodland Lake, and Devil's Thumb as well as Lost Lake. Take the one on your extreme left.

Expect to crisscross a couple of times over Middle Boulder Creek, passing Hessie Falls to your left and another set of waterfalls. Finally, you will reach Lost Lake.

Remember to stay on designated trails whenever possible. Do not take shortcuts, particularly when the route is wet, as doing so destroys vegetation and causes erosion. Because Lost Lake abuts the Indian Peaks Wilderness Area, but is not within its boundaries, you may have your dog off leash and under voice and sight command. However, if you take a short walk past the lake you will enter the IPWA where dogs must be on leash at all times.

Snow-covered mountains, Lost Lake, Hessie Townsite area

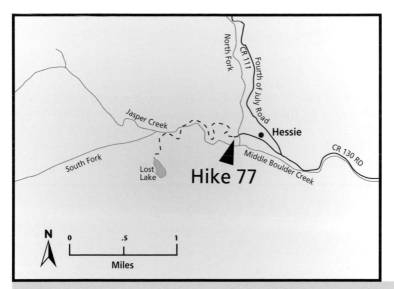

To the trailhead: Park alongside the road where permitted (for directions, see p. 230).

Distance: 2.8 miles round-trip

Difficulty: 780 feet

Elevation gain: Easy

Dogs: Yes, on leash at all times on IPWA land; otherwise under voice and sight command

Highlights: Pleasant hike through a forest; great hike to do with youngsters—make a game out of finding a "lost" lake

Jurisdiction: Boulder Ranger District, Arapaho and Roosevelt National Forests

King Lake

The trail to King Lake weaves through forests and meadows, briefly connects with the Devil's Thumb Bypass and Woodland Lake Trails, and cuts past treeline to the high alpine tundra dotted with wildflowers. At the end of the 6 mile trail, you'll find regal King Lake at 9,624 feet. A near-perfect circle, the lake glows blue-green and sits 300 feet below Rollins Pass.

Although anglers and some hikers reach the lake via Moffat Road, a more scenic and aerobic route is from the Hessie Townsite.

Starting from the Hessie Trailhead, walk west over a bridge crossing Middle Boulder Creek's North Fork and into the forest. Look for a large trailhead kiosk with maps of the various trails available: King Lake, Woodland Lake, and Lost Lake as well as Devil's Thumb. Take the one on your extreme left. Be sure not to veer right just before a large footbridge on the Devil's Thumb Bypass Trail. Although the trail is well-marked, stay left.

Expect a steady 4-mile or so climb along the South Fork of gushing Middle Boulder Creek. It's a long, pleasant ascent with few trail junctions

Heading down to King Lake, King Lake Trail, Continental Divide

Opposite: Paintbrush and columbine, King Lake Trail, Continental Divide

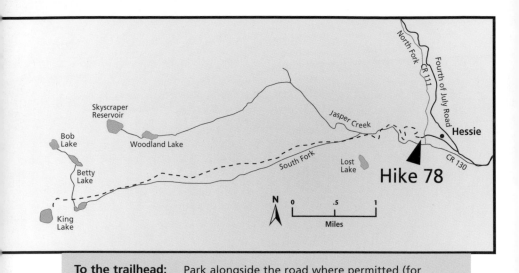

To the trailhead:	Park alongside the road where permitted (for directions, see p. 230).
Distance:	12 miles round-trip
Difficulty:	Moderate to strenuous because of distance
Elevation gain:	2,431 feet
Dogs:	Yes, on leash at all times
Highlights:	Spectacular highland lake; fishing permitted (state license required)
Jurisdiction:	Boulder Ranger District, Arapaho and Roosevelt National Forests

as you enter the Indian Peaks Wilderness Area. The last 1.5 miles or so is steeper, traveling through a dense spruce forest and several open valleys.

Marshy, wet meadows flank parts of the path to King Lake. Hikers are advised to take their breaks in the forest along the lengthy trail rather than the open meadows because of swarming mosquitoes.

Just before treeline, the trail makes several switchbacks up a steep ridge leading out of the trees. Again, stay left and do not take a right turn off of the main trail. Veering right would lead you to Bob and Betty Lakes (see Hike 79, p. 237).

Just below the Continental Divide, King Lake sits in a cirque basin. Locate a large boulder and soak your feet in the icy water or extend your hike about 300 more feet up to the ridge and the junction of the Corona Trail.

Snap a few photos, have a snack, and return the way you came.

Bob and Betty Lakes

Like many trails in and around the Hessie Townsite, the trail to Bob and Betty Lakes scoots for miles into the highlands, offering great views and backpacking opportunities.

To access the long 5.7-mile trail to Bob and Betty Lakes from the Hessie Trailhead, walk west over a bridge crossing Middle Boulder Creek's North Fork and into the forest. Look for a large trailhead kiosk with maps of the various trails available: King Lake, Woodland Lake, Devil's Thumb and Lost Lake. Take the King Lake Trail on your extreme left.

The wide and rocky trail zigzags as it ascends a ridge. Listen closely for the rush and roar of a waterfall to your left as you walk about 10 minutes along the trail. The falls are tucked away from the footpath in the forest. Although you can hear the waterfall, you actually cannot see it from the trail.

Continue on to another large bridge and signposts at the Lost Lake Trail Junction. Cross this bridge on your left and follow King Lake Trail as it now

Alpine sunflowers, Betty Lake, Bob and Betty Lakes Trail

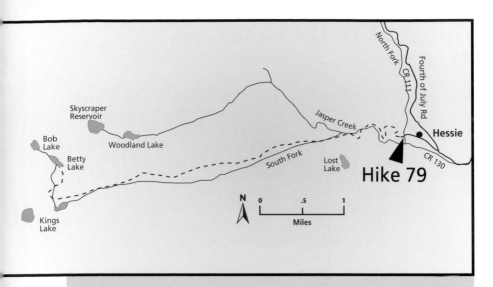

To the trailhead:	Park alongside the road where permitted (for directions, see p. 230).
Distance:	11.4 miles round-trip
Difficulty:	Strenuous
Elevation gain:	2,400 feet
Dogs:	Yes, on leash at all times
Highlights:	Duo of lovely small lakes; fishing permitted (state license required)
Jurisdiction:	Boulder Ranger District, Arapaho and Roosevelt National Forests

parallels the South Fork of Middle Boulder Creek along a sturdy variety of pine trees. As the trail ascends more steeply, you'll have to keep a keen eye out or else you risk losing sight of the footpath. Be sure to look for cairns while you walk along krummholz and willows to first Betty Lake, then Bob Lake about 200 feet higher to the northwest.

King Lake is farther south along the trail, on a more pronounced footpath. Look for Bob and Betty Lakes down and to your right as the clearly identifiable trail veers elsewhere toward King Lake.

Betty Lake sits just above treeline and from the sky it looks like a giant's footprint in the tundra. Bob Lake is much deeper and only a little larger than Betty Lake. Both allow fishing and are lovely to look at, but please don't swim here.

Jasper Lake to Devil's Thumb Lake

A hike to kidney-shaped Jasper Lake nurtures the soul like so many other backcountry experiences.

To start the 5.5-mile hike, begin at the Hessie Trailhead, crossing the foot bridge to access the Devil's Thumb Trail. The gently sloping trail follows an old service road along the south side of a roaring creek. The route is well-marked with a few steep stretches.

Dandelions and waterfall, Jasper Lake outlet, Jasper Lake to Devil's Thumb Lake Trail

After about 1 mile you'll come upon the Lost Lake Trail Junction. Stay right. From here is a flat 0.2 mile to the King Lake Trail connection, but again stay on the Devil's Thumb Trail.

You'll soon enter a high mountain valley dotted with colorful wildflowers during the summer months. From here it is 3 miles or so, offering an intermittent gentle incline through the forest and riparian woodland weaving its way to Jasper Lake. This is a good place to take a break and evaluate your progress. Scenic photo opportunities exist here as well.

The trail continues another 1 mile from Jasper Lake, passes a couple of tarns, and leads to Devil's Thumb Lake. This lake lies at timberline, just below the Devil's Thumb.

Ambitious hikers might opt to continue about 2 miles to the steep and rocky Devil's Thumb Pass (elevation 11,747). From the pass you can see the Never Summer and Gore Mountain Ranges to the north and west. The Continental Divide stands tall, exactly 2 miles from Jasper Lake.

Proximity, beauty, and variety are the words that best characterize the Jasper Lake to Devil's Thumb Lake hiking experience.

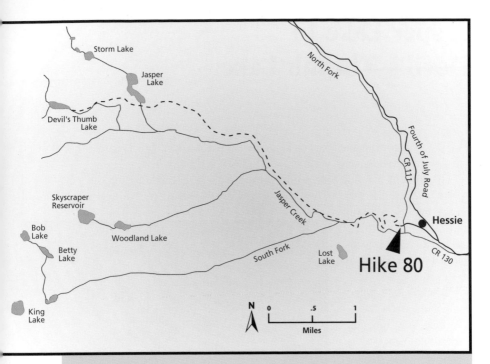

Storm Lake
Jasper Lake
Devil's Thumb Lake
North Fork
Fourth of July Road
CR 111
Hessie
Skyscraper Reservoir
Bob Lake
Woodland Lake
Jasper Creek
Betty Lake
South Fork
Lost Lake
Hike 80
CR 130
King Lake

N
0   .5   1
Miles

To the trailhead:	Park alongside the road where permitted.
Distance:	11 miles round-trip
Difficulty:	Moderate to strenuous because of distance
Elevation gain:	2,131 feet
Dogs:	Yes, on leash at all times
Highlights:	Kidney-shaped lake stocked with cutthroat, brook, and brown trout; fishing allowed (state license required); camping requires permit
Jurisdiction:	Boulder Ranger District, Arapaho and Roosevelt National Forests

Opposite: Approach to Jasper Lake, Jasper Lake to Devil's Thumb Lake Trail, Hessie Townsite area

Skyscraper Reservoir

Skyscraper Reservoir sits just above timberline at 11,221 feet. Cutthroat trout are stocked in the cold lake that is about 28-feet deep at its deepest spot.

The trail to Skyscraper Reservoir is relatively easy, gaining just enough elevation to make you feel like you've done some exercise. Advancing barely under 2,000 feet, fit and focused visitors hiking at a consistent pace can expect to reach the sparkling lake in about an hour and a half.

To reach Skyscraper Reservoir, start at the Hessie Trailhead and take the Devil's Thumb Trail—not the bypass—west for 2.3 miles where it hooks up with Woodland Lake Trail. Keep to the right, and be sure not to veer left onto the King Lake Trail (see Hike 78, p. 234).

The Woodland Creek Trail follows a drainage, crisscrossing lively Middle Boulder Creek, and traverses through swampy lowlands and open rocky meadows. Following a glistening stream on the south side of the trail, you'll enter a varied forest canopy of spruce and fir. Look closely: Dilapidated cabins appear buried in the forest and you may see an occasional black bear munching from a raspberry bush.

Shoreline grasses and views of the Continental Divide, Woodland Lake, Skyscraper Reservoir Trail

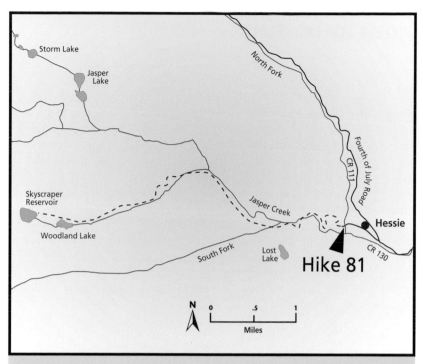

To the trailhead:	Park alongside the road where permitted (for directions, see p. 230).
Distance:	5.6 miles round-trip
Difficulty:	Easy to moderate
Elevation gain:	1,727
Dogs:	Yes, on leash at all times
Highlights:	Wooded trail; nice outing for novice hikers
Jurisdiction:	Boulder Ranger District, Arapaho and Roosevelt National Forests

On your way you'll pass Woodland Lake, which is smaller than Skyscraper Reservoir. Woodland Lake is nestled in about 60 yards to the left of the trail. Rest here or continue on a moderate incline west of Woodland Lake up to Skyscraper Reservoir. Rock cairns will guide your way.

Fourth of July

What a peculiar name: Fourth of July Trail. Many people actually do seek out this hike during the month of July because of the plentiful and vivid wildflowers all along the route. Ute and Arapaho tribes established successful hunting camps all along this area. Careful excavations have revealed ancient steam pits and game drive walls nearby. If you find an artifact, leave it intact and report it to the Boulder Ranger District.

From the Fourth of July Trailhead, the rocky and unassuming dirt trail weaves through fragrant spruce and fir forests with small creeks cutting through the trail, causing the footpath to be muddy in spots. Please be mindful to stay on the trail, in spite of the mud. Walking off trail causes erosion and needlessly tramples sensitive vegetation.

To reach the Fourth of July Trailhead, from the Hessie Townsite (see p. 230), veer right on Hessie Road (CR 111). Continue approximately 7 miles, dead-ending at Buckingham Campground.

Diamond Lake

The towering summits of the Indian Peaks Wilderness Area, hardy old-growth forests, and several icy waterfalls distinguish the trail leading to sparkling Diamond Lake.

The lake sits high with a large grassy meadow to the north and south, framed by snowcapped mountains, and is home to many fish. Diamond Lake is stocked with rainbow, cutthroat, and brook trout.

To begin the short 2-mile hike, start at the Fourth of July Trailhead near Buckingham Campground. At the large wooden kiosk, take the Arapaho Pass Trail. You'll hike along the Arapaho Pass Trail for about 1 mile in the spruce-fir forest.

The trail is somewhat wet in areas because of several small streams flowing down the slope to the creek at the valley floor. Expect to rock-hop across water in a few spots. You'll soon come to the Diamond Lake Trail junction, veering left while the Arapaho Pass Trail leads steeply up and to your right.

The Diamond Lake Trail weaves and drops about 250 feet into the North Fork of Middle Boulder Creek. You'll cross this rushing creek on a double-log footbridge. A spectacular waterfall is on your right and numerous huge boulders are strewn about.

The last stretch of the trail opens up into a spacious marshy meadow peppered with flowers during the summer. A couple of dense snowfields may still exist as late as July.

Golden retrievers and waterfall, Diamond Lake Trail, Fourth of July area

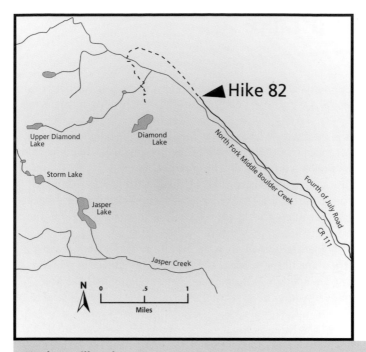

Hike 82

Upper Diamond Lake

Diamond Lake

North Fork Middle Boulder Creek

Fourth of July Road

Storm Lake

CR 111

Jasper Lake

Jasper Creek

N

0   .5   1

Miles

To the trailhead:	The trailhead is west of the Buckingham Campground. Parking accommodates about 20 to 25 vehicles (for directions, see p. 244).
Distance:	4 miles round-trip
Difficulty:	Easy to moderate
Elevation gain:	951 feet
Dogs:	Yes, on leash at all times
Highlights:	Wetlands area; camping nearby; fishing permitted (state license required)
Jurisdiction:	Boulder Ranger District, Arapaho and Roosevelt National Forests

With its clear, sparkling water, Diamond Lake sits quietly just below treeline. This is a near-perfect lunch spot where you can observe anglers standing along the shoreline. Return as you ascended or explore along the trail that leads about two-thirds of the way around the lake.

Fourth of July Mine

This hike is a beautiful trek to a century-old mine. The Fourth of July Mine was set up by C.C. Alvord in 1875, after he discovered silver, but little gold, in the area. The mine is located south and west of Boulder's primary water source, Arapaho Glacier. (This is Colorado's largest glacier, sitting south and east of the Continental Divide.)

To access the Fourth of July Mine, begin on the Arapaho Pass Trail from the Fourth of July Trailhead at the west end of Buckingham Campground, and hike into the forest.

The ascent doesn't feel like it ever lets up as it climbs the wooded, northern slope of the North Fork of the Middle Boulder Creek drainage. Enjoy the high mountain valley, with its clear air, and don't think about the exhausting effort.

As you continue through the woods, crossing streams on stepping stones as necessary, you'll eventually intersect the Diamond Lake Trail in 1.2 miles. Do not take this fork to the left, but rather turn right on the steep switchback, staying on the Arapaho Pass Trail.

Monkshood and larkspur, Fourth of July Trail, Fourth of July area

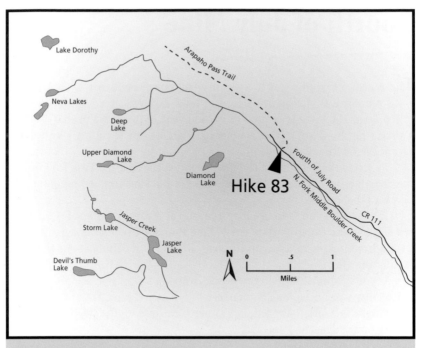

Lake Dorothy

Arapaho Pass Trail

Neva Lakes

Deep Lake

Upper Diamond Lake

Diamond Lake

Hike 83

Fourth of July Road

N. Fork Middle Boulder Creek

CR 111

Jasper Creek

Storm Lake

Jasper Lake

Devil's Thumb Lake

N

0   .5   1

Miles

To the trailhead:	The trailhead is west of the Buckingham Campground (for directions, see p. 244).
Distance:	4.2 miles round-trip
Difficulty:	Moderate
Elevation gain:	1,145 feet
Dogs:	Yes, on leash at all times
Highlights:	Historic landmark; panoramic views; site of ancient Native American camps
Jurisdiction:	Boulder Ranger District, Arapaho and Roosevelt National Forests

The route offers up really expansive views, reaching the mine in another mile. The Fourth of July Mine ruins, at 11,245 feet, are located on a wide, flat bench, 2.1 miles from the trailhead, directly north of the trail that turns off to access the Arapaho Glacier Trail. After exploring the area and perhaps having a snack, return the way you came.

South Arapaho Peak

South Arapaho Peak stands rugged at 13,397 feet, and the ramble up the trail is some 3,200 vertical feet on a moderate and pleasant incline.

Begin the hike at the Fourth of July Trailhead west of the Buckingham Campground. Spruce and fir needles litter the forest floor. Along the first section of the clearly marked trail, the ground is spongy and black, crisscrossed with knotty tree roots, lending an almost spooky air of mystery and intrigue.

Several flowing creeks cut through the trail farther up. The small creeks, sparkling in the sunlight and few in number, are easily crossed by rock-hopping. At about 11,300 feet, head right at the sign indicating Arapaho Glacier, rather than veering left to Arapaho Pass.

Nearly an hour or so along the Arapaho Glacier Trail, standing desolate in a spacious high-mountain meadow, you'll come upon a strikingly tall cairn made of various-size rocks. From this point, it is less than 1,000 feet to the summit.

From a saddle at 12,770 feet, look down to the north for views of Arapaho Glacier. The rocks bordering Arapaho Glacier are polished by the movement of ice. The water pooling with floating chunks of ice in the valley below glows blue-gray. Common sense dictates that one would not climb down near the glacier or hike beyond the Arapaho Glacier Overlook.

There's a windbreak shelter made of rock here for those wanting to rest and maybe take a few photos before the final ascent to the top. Although there is not a trail, the summit remains in clear view as you climb to the left. From the saddle up to the summit of South Arapaho Peak is an easy, yet steep, rock scramble. The glacier and peak itself are a part of the City of Boulder watershed.

Marsh marigold, South Arapaho Peak, viewed from Diamond Lake Trail, Fourth of July area

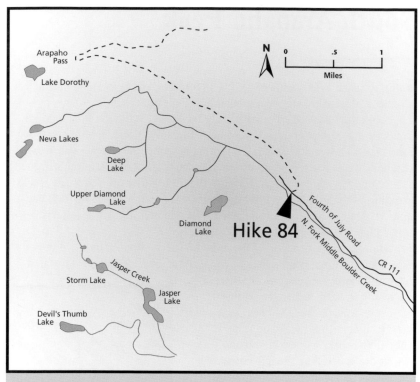

Arapaho Pass

Lake Dorothy

Neva Lakes

Deep Lake

Upper Diamond Lake

Diamond Lake

Hike 84

Fourth of July Road

N. Fork Middle Boulder Creek

CR 111

N

0   .5   1

Miles

Jasper Creek

Storm Lake

Jasper Lake

Devil's Thumb Lake

To the trailhead:	The trailhead is west of the Buckingham Campground (for directions, see p. 244).
Distance:	8 miles round-trip
Difficulty:	Moderate to strenuous
Elevation gain:	3,200 feet
Dogs:	Yes, on leash at all times
Highlights:	Columbine grow along the trail; unusually large cairn marks the way farther up
Jurisdiction:	Boulder Ranger District, Arapaho and Roosevelt National Forests

On a clear day from the summit, you can see Pikes Peak way to the south and a great deal of eastern Colorado. If time and weather permit, ambitious hikers may opt to go an additional hour or so to the summit of nearby North Arapaho Peak, climbing carefully along a rocky, narrow ridge.

Allenspark

Allenspark is today a quiet residential village, and for that reason, outsiders to the area should be courteous when traveling through and accessing published trailheads.

At an elevation of 8,450 feet, the tiny town located between Lyons and Estes Park has a population of less than a 1,000 citizens. Their residences were no doubt chosen because of the inspiring scenery and rare glimpses of fleeting wildflowers and elusive animals.

The U.S. Postal Service spells it Allenspark and the National Park Service and U.S. Geological Survey spell it Allens Park. Whichever way you choose to spell it, drive slowly and carefully when accessing trails in this quaint and charming area.

St. Vrain Mountain

The mountain, river, glacier, and other places bearing the name St. Vrain are in memory of early traders to the area, Ceran and his brother Marcellin St. Vrain.

This hike takes you to the edge of southeastern Rocky Mountain National Park. It's demanding, gaining 3,262 vertical feet in 4.7 miles, but the panoramic views in all directions from St. Vrain's summit are breathtaking.

The trail starts in a thicket of aspen and lodgepole pine. After about 20 minutes or so, depending on your pace, you will enter the Indian Peaks Wilderness Area. Dogs must be on leash at all times in the wilderness area.

The route climbs 2 miles gradually along a lateral glacial moraine following numerous tight switchbacks. It eventually opens up in an old forest fire area.

The footpath breaks out of treeline into a wide open meadow scattered with krummholz. Here, at 11,632 feet, you'll spot Meadow Mountain to your right (north), an easy scramble along the rocks, and the summit of St. Vrain standing tall to the south and west, at 12,162 feet.

Eastern foothills, Saint Vrain Mountain Trail, Allenspark

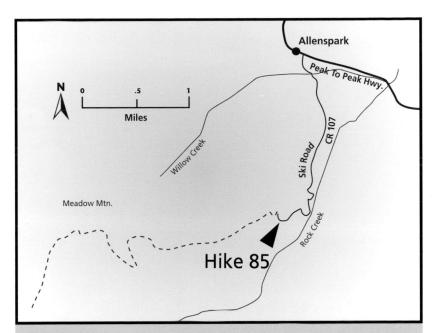

To the trailhead:	Take US 36 north from Boulder to Lyons. Turn left (west) on CO 7 to Ferncliffe and take the business loop to Ski Road (CR 107). Turn left (south) and drive about 0.5 mile, then turn left (east), eventually coming to a fork. Veer right and follow it to the St. Vrain Mountain Trailhead.
Distance:	9 miles round-trip
Difficulty:	Moderate to strenuous
Elevation gain:	3,262 feet
Dogs:	Yes, on leash at all times
Highlights:	Adequate trailhead parking; spacious high mountain valley
Jurisdiction:	Boulder Ranger District, Arapaho and Roosevelt National Forests

As you walk along this trail, **Saint Vrain Mountain Trail, Allenspark** you will see signs informing you that you are entering the perimeter of Rocky Mountain National Park. Dogs are not allowed anywhere in the park, so if you've brought along your pet, you must turn around at this point or veer further east to access St. Vrain Mountain from the south. You may also opt to climb Meadow Mountain, now behind you, instead.

As you continue on, you exit Rocky Mountain National Park after about 0.5 a mile. There are signs indicating when you exit the park lands as well as when you enter.

From this saddle, climb 0.7 mile south along the trail through mixed tundra. You'll lose the trail but it's easy to see the summit about 700 feet above, so pick any route you choose, being careful not to trample on the fragile alpine tundra.

Peaceful Valley

Camping. Picnicking. Nature walks. The aptly named Peaceful Valley region invites all sorts of passive and active uses. The high meadow stands serene, abutting the Peak-to-Peak Scenic Byway.

Flanked by Rocky Mountain National Park to the north and west and Boulder to the south and east, the Peaceful Valley area owes more than beauty and bracing climate to its high-altitude setting. The mountains bring fragrance of spruce from their forests and icy highland lakes and streams dot the landscape. In about 1934, men from the Civilian Conservation Corps, working from camps at Peaceful Valley, built nearly 50 miles of trail in what is now the Indian Peaks Wilderness Area as well as road and forest improvements.

To hike in and around the Peaceful Valley area, with its numerous trail connections, is to experience the epitome of Colorado's nobility and wild beauty.

Buchanan Pass Trail

Undoubtedly one of the most picturesque and peaceful hikes next to and entering the Indian Peaks Wilderness Area is the Buchanan Pass Trail. Hiking, bicycling, skiing, or snowshoeing along this rugged high-country eastern stretch invigorates even the most sedentary of us.

The trail spans some 16 miles from its eastern end near the Peaceful Valley and Camp Dick Campgrounds to its junction with the Cascade Creek Trail to the west. While about 5 miles of the Buchanan Pass Trail is outside of the IPWA and mountain bikes are allowed, the remaining western portion lies on National Forest land, in the jurisdiction of the Boulder Ranger District.

Along a consistent, gentle uphill slope, this approximately 4.3-mile section of the route heading westward begins left of the road past the Camp Dick Campground just off of the Peak-to-Peak Highway.

The trail is well-marked with tagged trees and few turns. The densely forested route offers access to the North Sourdough Trail immediately to your left (south). The Sourdough Trail (see Hike 76, p. 227) stretches some 14 miles due south, past the Brainard Lake Recreation Area all the way to the Rainbow Lakes Road near the University of Colorado Mountain Research Station. However, keep going due west and slightly north the entire way.

The footpath parallels the north side of Middle St. Vrain Creek. After about 4 miles or so, turn around at the junction of the St. Vrain Mountain Trail to your right (see Hike 85, p. 252) and return the way you came, completing an approximately 8.6-mile circuit.

Opposite: Lush pine forest, Buchanan Pass Trail, Brainard Lake area

The trail extends quite a bit farther west up to Gibraltar Lake, the source of Middle St. Vrain Creek, if you continue north and west along the St. Vrain Glacier Trail.

Buchanan Pass Trail, Brainard Lake area

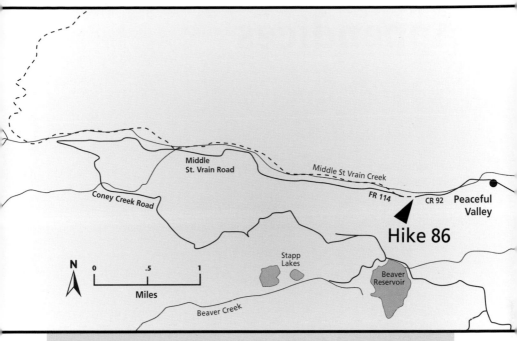

To the trailhead: From Boulder, take US 36 north to Lyons. From Lyons, take SR 7 west to the Peak-to-Peak Highway (CO 72). Turn left (south) to mile marker 50. Drive west about 4 miles onto FDR 114 through the Peaceful Valley and Camp Dick campgrounds.

Distance: 8.6 miles round-trip

Difficulty: Moderate

Elevation gain: 1,200 feet

Dogs: Yes, on leash at all times

Highlights: Not usually heavily traveled; plentiful trail connections

Jurisdiction: Boulder Ranger District, Arapaho and Roosevelt National Forests

Appendices

A. Land Management Jurisdictions

Arapaho and Roosevelt National Forests and Pawnee National Grassland
240 W. Prospect Road
Fort Collins, CO 80526
970-498-1100
www.fs.fed.us/r2/arnf/

Boulder County Parks & Open Space
P.O. Box 471
Boulder, CO 80306
303-441-3950
www.co.boulder.co.us/openspace

Boulder Ranger District, U.S. Forest Service
Visitor Information Center
2140 Yarmouth Ave.
Boulder, CO 80301
303-541-2500
www.fs.fed.us/r2/arnf/about/organization/brd/index.shtml

City of Boulder Open Space & Mountain Parks Department
P.O. Box 791
Boulder, CO 80306
303-441-3440
www.ci.boulder.co.us/openspace

The City of Boulder Parks and Recreation Department
3198 Broadway
Boulder, CO 80306
303-413-7200
www.ci.boulder.co.us/parks-recreation

City of Longmont, Button Rock Ranger Station
Button Rock Preserve
303-774-4300 ext. 4180
http://www.ci.longmont.co.us/water_waste/water/button_rock.htm

Estes Valley Recreation and Park District
P.O. Box 1379
Estes Park, CO 80517
970-586-8191
www.estesvalleyrecreation.com

Rocky Mountain National Park
1000 Hwy. 36
Estes Park, CO 80517
970-586-1206
www.nps.gov/romo

B. Other Outdoor Organizations

Leave No Trace Center for Outdoor Ethics
P.O. Box 997
Boulder, CO 80306
303-442-8222
800-332-4100 toll free
www.LNT.org

Colorado Division of Wildlife
6060 Broadway
Denver, CO 80216
303-297-1192
www.wildlife.state.co.us

Colorado Mountain Club, Boulder Group
Table Mesa Shopping Center
633 South Broadway, Unit N
Boulder, CO 80305
303-554-7688
www.cmcboulder.org

C. Hiker-Speak
A Glossary Of Trail Terms

Basin: An area of land drained by a river and its tributaries.

Bushwhack: Clearing a path through thick woods and shrubs, destroying low branches and bushes.

Cairn: A heap of stones piled up, usually in the shape of a pyramid, to mark your way. Some believe it is good luck to add a stone as you pass by.

Canyon: A deep valley with steep sides, often with a stream or river flowing through it.

Cirque: A deep, steep-walled basin on a mountain.

Continental Divide: The ridge of mountains in North America separating the streams that flow west into the Pacific Ocean from those that flow east into the Atlantic Ocean. Also called the Great Divide, this high-altitude area follows the crest of the Rocky Mountains from Canada to South America.

Couloir: An open gully.

Flatirons: Boulder's dramatic 300-million-year-old red sandstone slabs, resembling an old-fashioned clothes iron ("flatiron") standing on its end.

Fourteener: A mountain with an elevation higher than 14,000 feet above sea level.

Glacier: A large body of ice spreading outward along land.

Gulch: A deep ravine.

Krummholz: German for "crooked wood," those gnarled little trees that grow at higher elevations in the lee of boulders.

Meadow: A level area made up of grassland.

Mesa: Spanish for "table," an elevated landscape that is relatively flattopped.

Moraine: Gravel, rocks, and sand carried by glacial movement.

Saddle: A pass or ridge between two higher elevations or mountains.

Switchback: A zigzag or sharp turn on the trail, usually present along a steep rise.

Talus: A slope of rock debris.

Tarn: Of Scandinavian origin (tjörn), a small steep-banked mountain lake or pond.

Treeline: The upper limit of where trees grow at higher altitudes (also called timberline).

Tundra: The land above treeline, made up of mosses, lichens, and dwarf shrubs.

Valley: A low point between mountains, sometimes drained by a river.

Boulder Creek, City of Boulder

Selected Bibliography

Boddie, Caryn and Pete. *Hiking in Colorado.* Helena, MT.: Falcon Press Publishing Co., Inc., 1991.

Colorado Mountain Club Boulder Group. *Trail Map: Boulder Mountain Parks and Nearby Open Space.* Boulder, CO.: CMC Boulder Group, 2004.

Crutchfield, James. *It Happened in Colorado.* Guilford, CT.: Globe Pequot Press, 1993.

Cushman, Ruth Carol and Glenn. *Boulder Hiking Trails, 2nd edition.* Boulder, CO.: Pruett Publishing, 1999.

Dannen, Kent and Donna. *Hiking Rocky Mountain National Park.* Guilford, CT.: Globe Pequot Press, 2002.

Erickson, Bette. *Forever Young, a Hiking Guide.* Broomfield, CO.: CG Press, 2003.

Erickson, Bette. *Just For Little Legs: Family Hikes with Children.* Boulder, CO.: Westcliffe Publishers, 2008.

Erickson, Bette. *Just For the Challenge: Hikes with Bragging Rights.* Boulder, CO.: Westcliffe Publishers, 2008.

Erickson, Bette. *Just For Visitors: Where the Locals Hike.* Boulder, CO.: Westcliffe Publishers, 2008.

Erickson, Bette. *Just For the 2 of You: Romantic Hikes to Share.* Boulder, CO.: Westcliffe Publishers, 2008.

Fielder, John. *John Fielder's Best of Colorado.* Boulder, CO.: Westcliffe Publishers, 2009.

Irwin, Pamela and David Harlan. *100 Best Denver Area and Front Range Day Hikes.* Boulder, CO.: Westcliffe Publishers, 2003.

Roach, Jerry. *Colorado's Fourteeners, Companion Map Package.* Golden, CO.: Fulcrum Publishing, 1999. Actinella, Woolly, 224

Opposite: South Boulder Creek, Streamside Trail, Eldorado Canyon State Park

Index

mountains, 15, 148, 150
Mount Audubon hike, 215m, 224–226, 226m
Mount Meeker hike, 149m, 204–206, 206m
Mount Sanitas hike, 71m, 114–115, 114m

N
Nelson Loop Trail, 129, 130
Nelson Ranch, 130
Neva, Mount, 220p
Nighthawk Trail, 129, 130, 137
North Fork Shanahan Trail, 76
North Longs Peak Trail, 177
North Pella, 60
North Saint Vrain Creek, 133p
North Sourdough Trail, 256
Norwell family, 196
Nymph, Dream, and Bear Lakes hike, Emerald Lake via, 149m, 181–182, 182m

O
Olde Stage Fire of 1990, 55
Orodell, 28
Otis Peak, 166p, 168p
Ouzel Falls, 208p
Ouzel Falls hike, 149m, 207–209, 209m
Overland Mail Stage, 38

P
Parry primrose, 11p, 14p
Pawnee Pass Trail, 217, 220
Peaceful Valley, 255
Pella, 60
Pella Crossing hike, 25m, 60–62, 62m
Picture Rock, 120
Pines-to-Peak Trail, 121
Pioneer Trail, 52
Platts, Harlow, 48
Ponderosa Loop Trail, 126, 127

R
Rabbit Mountain hike, 71m, 131–132, 132m
Ralph Price Reservoir, 137–138
Ranger Trail, 90, 108
Range View-Ute Loop hike, 71m, 96–98, 98m
Rattlesnake Gulch Trail, 83
Red Rock Lake, 225p
Red Rocks "hogback" formation, 52p
Red Rocks Trail, 51, 52
Ribbon Falls, 173p
Ribbon Falls hike, 149m, 173–175, 175m
Roaring River, 160p
Rock Creek Farm, 37–39
Rock Creek Trail, 35
Rocky Mountain beeplant, 109p
Rocky Mountain National Park, 151–153
Royal Arch, 91p
Royal Arch hike, Chautauqua Park to, 71m, 89–91, 90m

S
Saddle Rock Trail, 90
safety, 19, 150
Sage Trail, 59
Sanitas Valley Trail, 115
Sawhill and Walden Ponds hike, 25m, 66–67, 67m
Sawhill Ponds, 66p
Settlers Park, 51
Settlers Park hike, 25m, 52–53, 53m
Shadow Canyon, 79p
Shanahan North and South Trails hike, 71m, 76–77, 77m
Ships Prow, 199p
Shirt Tail Peak, 81p
Skunk Canyon hike, 71m, 94–95, 94m
Skunk Canyon Trail, 86
Sky Pond hike, 149m, 179–180, 180m
Skyscraper Reservoir hike, 215m, 242–243, 243m

About the Author

Bette Erickson is an outdoor enthusiast, writer, and councilmember for the City and County of Broomfield. She has hiked, skied, and camped for more than 20 years throughout Colorado and elsewhere in the world.

Bette is a member of the Colorado Mountain Club, the Sierra Club, and the National League of Cities Institute for Youth, Education and Families. She and her husband, Paul Beaty, are Indian Peaks Wilderness Area Backcountry Volunteers. A former public school teacher, when not hiking Bette writes for numerous newspapers and magazines.

About the Photographers

Boulder residents Russell and Gail Dohrmann are avid photographers. Their favorite photographic subjects are travel, scenic, romantic, and creative, as well as flowers and still life. They enjoy combining their photography with their outdoor activities: hiking, cross-country skiing, and bicycling. Russell and

Gail are members of several Colorado arts and photography organizations, including the Boulder Art Association and Flatirons Photography Club. Their work has been published in magazines, calendars, cards, and books. A photo essay on fall in Colorado appeared in *Country Magazine*. They also exhibit their print photography at local and regional photography and art shows, where they have been recognized for their work.